Contents

Introduction

Academic Writing Skills 3 presents the skills necessary to write coherent, accurate, and logical university-level essays. There are four units in the textbook, each covering an important element of successful academic writing.

Unit 1 focuses on the pre-writing steps which prepare the writer to write an essay that efficiently accomplishes a desired task. Advanced concepts introduced include:

- interpreting a complex essay prompt.
- doing research before taking a position.

Unit 2 focuses on writing effective paragraphs, from the introduction to the conclusion. Advanced concepts introduced include:

- establishing a motive for the essay.
- building a paragraph around researched information.
- avoiding mistakes with logic.

Unit 3 focuses on outside sources, from selecting which sources to use to incorporating them effectively. Advanced concepts introduced include:

- distinguishing primary, secondary, and tertiary sources.
- sorting out the complexity of APA citation style.
- using a variety of reporting verbs to improve style.

Unit 4 focuses on improving the academic tone of an essay, with tips on language and editing. Advanced concepts introduced include:

- using hedging and intensifying to convey information more accurately.
- using conjunctions to improve cohesion.
- positioning information strategically using the passive form and nominalizations.
- efficiently editing an essay using a multi-step process.

To maximize the use of this book, you should:

- read the information in each unit thoroughly.
- take notes in the page margins on explanations from your teacher, classmates' comments, or your own thoughts.
- complete all the exercises.

UNIT

1

Preparing to Write

Part 1 Understanding the essay prompt

Part 2 Taking a position

Part 3 Doing research

Part 4 Planning the essay

Part 1

Understanding the essay prompt

Section 1 Identifying the requirements

Academic writing is the result of a process involving the research and careful consideration of a topic. The ultimate purpose of this process is for a writer to present a point of view on a topic that readers will accept as true or plausible. Writers must research their topic in order to present a point of view that is supported by logical and objective evidence.

Planning to write academically begins with the genre of the essay because this affects the organization of the essay. Common essay genres include argumentative, compare and contrast, or problem-solution essays (see Appendix A on page 130 for more on essay genres). The genre is often indicated by the words used in the essay prompt.

Therefore, since researching a topic is often guided by the requirements of an instruction, or essay prompt, it is essential that an academic writer considers:

What is the essay prompt asking me to do?

To understand the essay prompt, first identify its two main parts:

1. **the general topic**
2. **requirements for the essay**

Consider this prompt:

Analyze the growth of Apple's market share since the introduction of the iMac.

The general topic is *Apple, Inc*. The requirement for the essay is to *analyze the growth of market share since the introduction of the iMac.*

Requirements for the essay

After identifying the topic, the writer should look for requirements in the essay prompt. These requirements tell the writer what must be included in the essay.

There are four types of requirements in many prompts:

1. **Recall** – show knowledge learned from a reading, lecture, or some other source.

2. **Analysis** – break down a topic into smaller parts and explain the significance of each part.
3. **Synthesis** – use information from two or more sources (lectures, readings, etc.) to show a relationship and possible deeper meaning.
4. **Evaluation** – judge the value of something based on an analysis of information.

These requirements are often indicated by the use of certain instructional words in the essay prompt. Here is a list of common instructional words.

Requirement	Instructional words	Example
Recall	summarize list identify describe illustrate define	*Summarize the most significant theories of early twentieth century psychologists and how they revolutionized the field of psychology.* *Describe the American judicial system and how it is designed to limit wrongful convictions.* *Define the term "success" using points from the various assigned readings on Buddhism.*
Analysis	analyze examine discuss compare contrast determine	*Analyze the growth of Apple's market share since the introduction of the iMac.* *Discuss some of the advances in twentieth century technology which have helped transform the workplace.* *Compare the health care systems of France and the United States.*
Synthesis	use refer include incorporate	*Using points from the various readings assigned this semester, determine the most critical turning points in the evolution of human societies.* *Watch the film* Mulholland Drive *and identify its "film noir" characteristics. Refer to the aspects of the classic movies from the 1950s covered in the lecture.*
Evaluation	evaluate assess judge argue recommend comment	*Evaluate the effectiveness of anti-piracy laws on curbing the illegal downloading of digitalized video, music, and print.* *Argue for or against the expansion of the school week from five to seven days.*

NOTE: The writer is normally expected to express an objective opinion when the essay prompt asks for an evaluation. For other question types, an objective opinion is not normally expected. For example:

Compare the health care systems of France and the United States.

(No opinion asked for – the writer must only provide evidence to support how the two systems differ or are similar.)

Compare the health care systems of France and the United States. Then evaluate the more successful of the two in terms of overall public health.

(Opinion asked for – the writer must both provide evidence to support how the two systems differ or are similar, and express an objective opinion about these differences or similarities.)

Exercise 1

For each example essay prompt in the table on page 3:

a. underline the topic.

b. circle any instructional words indicating a requirement.

Example:

Analyze the growth of Apple's market share since the introduction of the iMac.

Section 2 Understanding longer essay prompts

Longer essay prompts with more details included are commonly assigned. In a longer essay prompt with multiple requirements, identifying the general topic may be a challenge. For example:

Many governments, for a variety of reasons, are seeking energy sources which can help them curb their reliance on fossil fuels. Assess how much countries should rely on nuclear energy to help meet this goal and their energy needs. Be sure to discuss matters of concern regarding energy use, such as cost and environmental impact, and make comparisons among various energy sources regarding these. Include statistics from a variety of sources to help support your position.

In the prompt above, what is the general topic?

a. Fossil fuels
b. Nuclear energy
c. Various energy sources

The correct answer is **b** – nuclear energy.

Identifying requirements in longer essay prompts

With longer essay prompts, the writer must be very clear about the different requirements. One way to do this is by identifying and circling each instructional word indicating a requirement. For example:

Many governments, for a variety of reasons, are seeking energy sources which can help them curb their reliance on fossil fuels. Assess how much countries should rely on nuclear energy to help meet this goal and their energy needs. Be sure to discuss matters of concern regarding energy use, such as cost and environmental impact, and make comparisons among various energy sources regarding these. Include statistics from a variety of sources to help support your position.

In this essay prompt, there are four clear requirements:

- *Assess how much countries should rely on nuclear energy to help meet this goal and their energy needs.*
- *Discuss matters of concern regarding energy use.*
- *Make comparisons among various energy sources.*
- *Include statistics from a variety of sources to help support your position.*

The main requirement is often the first one; it should be the focus of the entire essay. The other instructional words show sub-requirements (or even sub-sub-requirements) – the different levels of focus which the writer should include at some point in the essay.

To distinguish main from sub- and sub-sub-requirements, create an outline of the essay prompt, formatted as follows:

Main requirement
- Sub-requirement 1
    - Sub-sub-requirement
- Sub-requirement 2
    - Etc.

For example, an outline of the requirements from the essay prompt on nuclear energy could be:

Main requirement:	*Assess how much countries should rely on nuclear energy to help meet this goal and their energy needs.*
Sub-requirement 1:	*Discuss matters of concern regarding energy use.*
Sub-sub-requirement:	*Make comparisons among various energy sources.*
Sub-requirement 2:	*Include statistics from a variety of sources to help support your position.*

Exercise 2

Look at the essay prompts on the next page and:

a. underline the general topic.

b. circle any instructional words indicating a requirement.

c. outline the requirements to show the main from sub- and sub-sub-requirements.

1. Select several of Picasso's paintings representing both his pre- and post-war periods. Compare aspects of both periods. Explain the transformations which occurred in his art, making sure to refer to color, images, and expressions.

2. The lectures in this course have thus far focused on the 30 articles in the U.N. Declaration of Human Rights and the historical basis for each. Select one of the Declaration's member countries and describe the challenges it faces in trying to uphold the human rights standards outlined in the articles. Determine how close the country is to being a model human rights state.

3. In the class, examples were given of how socio-cultural factors affect the perception of certain issues which often lead to misunderstandings and breakdowns in diplomatic negotiations, protests, and even armed conflicts. Select a particular issue which eventually led to an armed conflict. Contrast how this issue may have been perceived on both sides of the conflict, making sure to include points on differing values, beliefs, behavior, and laws.

4. Analyze a contemporary novel with a female protagonist and compare and contrast it with classic works where women were traditionally portrayed as the villain or victim, such as in the works analyzed in the course (e.g., *Macbeth*, *The Scarlet Letter*, *The Great Gatsby*, *Washington Square*). Be sure to a) comment on whether or not women still come across as being the "weaker sex" in more modern literature, and b) identify where symbolism and allegory are used in defining the woman's character.

Part 2 Taking a position

Section 1 Choosing a position

For every essay prompt, the writer must take a position. This position is what the writer claims to be true about the topic. The entire essay should be focused on supporting this position. Therefore, a clear position helps ensure that the essay is coherent and organized.

The position a writer could take depends on the essay prompt. For example:

Do you agree or disagree with the following statement: "Globalization has had a positive influence on Asia"?

The topic is globalization. The position a writer could take on the topic seems to be limited to two options:

- It has had a positive influence on Asia.

OR

- It has not had a positive influence on Asia.

However, in an academic subject, it is rare that something is completely right or wrong, positive or negative, best or worst. Therefore, other positions on the topic of the essay prompt above could be:

- It has had a mostly positive influence on Asia.
- It has had a somewhat negative influence on Asia.
- It has had a positive influence in some sectors of societies in Asia but negative in others.
- Certain countries in Asia have benefitted more from globalization than others.

Other types of essay prompts do not ask for agreement or disagreement. For example:

When did the process of globalization start?

The topic again is globalization. Possible positions on the topic could be:

- It truly began with the advent of information technology.
- It is not a recent phenomenon but has a long history spanning millennia.
- It is impossible to determine when exactly it began, but it has certainly intensified over the last few decades.
- During the European era of exploration and conquest during the sixteenth and seventeenth centuries is when the world truly started to become globalized.

The following essay prompt is even more open:

Define globalization.

This kind of prompt asks the writer to use a particular approach in responding to the prompt. The approach taken is the writer's position. Different positions to the above essay prompt could be:

- Globalization is a set of processes that have made the world seem smaller.
- Globalization has increased the economic, cultural, and political links among countries.
- Globalization is a process that has increased the importance of a global shared culture and at the same time the importance of local cultures.
- Cultural, economic, and political connections have increased to such an extent that borders and differences among countries, cultures, and people have no meaning.

To summarize, for most essay prompts there is a variety of positions. The writer is free to choose any position as long as it:

- responds directly to the essay prompt.
- can be supported well, normally with research.

Exercise 1

Look at the essay prompts below. For each, list at least three possible positions a writer could take.

Essay prompt	Possible positions
1. Discuss some of the technological advances in the twentieth century which have helped transform the workplace.	
2. Compare the health care systems of France and the United States.	
3. Evaluate the effectiveness of anti-piracy laws on curbing the illegal downloading of digitalized video, music, and print.	
4. Argue for or against the expansion of the school week from five to seven days.	
5. Summarize the most significant developments in social networking and describe their impact on the lives of internet users today.	
6. Examine some of the most popular shows currently on TV and offer insights into why they are popular. Make comments on how the popularity of these shows may reflect certain characteristics of society.	

NOTE: The initial position a writer takes may change, especially if research shows that another position is more valid.

Part 3 Doing research

Section 1 Starting research

Academic essays are different from other types of essays because they include research. Below is the process many writers follow before writing the first draft of their essay:

Read essay prompt → Do research → Take position → Create outline

1. When to start research

In the process above, the writer does research immediately after reading the essay prompt. Since many academic topics are rather complex, the writer takes a position after gaining a better understanding of the topic through research. This helps ensure that the position is well informed and less biased.

In some cases, the writer may have some knowledge of the topic and take a position before researching. However, a writer who does not research all possible positions risks:

- ignoring or overlooking useful information.
- writing an essay that is biased.

2. Asking questions

After understanding the essay prompt, it is important to create a list of questions which will help guide research into the topic. These questions should:

- give the writer a better understanding of the topic.
- enable the writer to take an informed position based on the research.

In the essay prompt:

Analyze the growth of Apple's market share since the introduction of the iMac.

the instructional word "analyze" is used, so the writer needs to research such questions as:

- What were the statistics on Apple's market share growth prior to and since the introduction of the iMac?
- What factors have contributed to this growth?

In the longer essay prompt:

Many governments, for a variety of reasons, are seeking energy sources which can help them curb their reliance on fossil fuels. Assess how much countries should rely on nuclear energy to help meet this goal and their energy needs. Be sure to discuss matters of concern regarding energy use, such as cost and environmental impact, and make comparisons among various energy sources regarding these. Include statistics from a variety of sources to help support your position.

there are multiple requirements listed, but the main requirement is indicated with the instructional word "assess." The writer is expected to give an opinion on the topic. To form this opinion, the writer needs to research such questions as:

- What are the statistics on how much nuclear energy is currently used?
- What are the benefits and drawbacks of nuclear energy use?
- How do alternative energy sources compare with nuclear energy?

Exercise 1

Below are the essay prompts from page 9. For each prompt, create a list of questions to research.

Essay prompt	Research questions
1. Discuss some of the technological advances in the twentieth century which have helped transform the workplace.	
2. Compare the health care systems of France and the United States.	
3. Evaluate the effectiveness of anti-piracy laws on curbing the illegal downloading of digitalized video, music, and print.	
4. Argue for or against the expansion of the school week from five to seven days.	
5. Summarize the most significant developments in social networking and describe their impact on the lives of internet users today.	
6. Examine some of the most popular shows currently on TV and offer insights into why they are popular. Make comments on how the popularity of these shows may reflect certain characteristics of society.	

Section 2 Keeping a research list

It is important to keep a list of research which includes:

- information which could be used in the essay.
- the source of the information.

Here is a sample research list for the essay prompt on how much countries should rely on nuclear energy (page 11).

Information

Source (writer or title, page number)

- *Nuclear – 13.4% world energy supply* ("2011 Key world" 24)
- *Nuclear energy preferred in Asia* (Chang and Thomson 26)
- *301 new reactors under construction, planned, or proposed* ("Asia's Nuclear Energy")
- *British Energy: Torness nuclear reactor CO_2 emissions = 5 g/kWh, coal plant = 900 g/kWh* ("Environmental" 6)
- *Nuclear reactor's greenhouse gas emissions lower than wind and solar power* ("Technology")
- *Solar – one hour of sun's power = human energy needs for a year* ("Solar Power")
- *If innovation increased, solar can produce more energy* (Tanaka, "Solar"; Tanaka, "Technology")
- *After Fukushima, suspension / cancelling new nuclear plants "merely a knee-jerk reaction to stifle growing public hysteria over nuclear safety"* (Kimura 31)
- *Chernobyl, 1986, 31 immediate deaths, other radiation-related deaths later* (several sources)
- *Fatalities coal extraction – 20,000, hydropower – 30,000 deaths* (Nuclear Energy Agency)
- *Nuclear – 2.14 cents / kWh, natural gas – 4.86 cents / kWh, oil – 15.18 cents / kWh* ("Nuclear Energy Institute – Economic")
- *As solar power costs fall, will lead to increase at local level* (Roaf and Gupta 2009, pp. 84–107; Christopher, Kumar, et al. 2009, p. 9)
- *Solar power – expensive solar panels* ("Solar Power")
- *Stable sources of uranium available from Canada or Australia* ("Nuclear Power: Nukes of Hazard")
- *Nuclear reactor Britain estimated $7.9 billion* ("Nuclear Power: Nukes of Hazard")

Section 3 Synthesizing research

Writers analyze the information they gain from research in order to take an informed position on a topic. Part of this analysis is synthesizing related ideas to make a statement about the topic. For example, research for the essay prompt:

Analyze the growth of Apple's market share since the introduction of the iMac.

may have revealed the following information:

- The Apple name and logo were appealing and contrasted with the colder, more machine-like image of IBM. (Kluger)
- "On May 6, 1998, Steve Jobs unveiled the iMac, a desktop computer whose translucent, brightly colored shell made it instantly distinctive from other PCs on the market … its success was critical in reviving the company's fortunes." (*Apple: A history …*)
- "Thanks to its sleek, simple interface and the fact it allowed users to tote their entire music library in one device in their pocket, the iPod transformed how we buy and listen to music." (*Apple: A history …*)

A synthesis of the researched information above may lead the writer to state the following:

Design was a major reason Apple's products and brand image became attractive to consumers.

Research may have also revealed the following information:

- Apple has hundreds of retail stores around the world which sell products directly to consumers – this helps eliminate the cost of paying a middleman to distribute the product. (Hiner)
- Apple is able to source components at a discounted rate, which enables them to manufacture products at a fraction of what it would normally cost to produce a new technologically advanced product. (Gobry)
- Apple earns close to a 60% profit margin on each sale of the iPhone, far higher than for competitors. (Elmer-DeWitt)

By synthesizing the above information, a possible statement about Apple could be:

Apple's manufacturing and distribution process enables the company to earn a relatively high profit on each product sold.

Exercise 2

Analyze the research list on page 13 and:

- identify pieces of information on the list which are related to each other and write them in the table below.
- synthesize the information and then write a statement about the essay topic based on this research information in the table below.

Research information: Synthesis statement:
Research information: Synthesis statement:
Research information: Synthesis statement:

Exercise 3

Read the following essay prompt and possible positions. Choose the position that is best supported by the information synthesized in Exercise 2.

> Many governments, for a variety of reasons, are seeking energy sources which can help them curb their reliance on fossil fuels. Assess how much countries should rely on nuclear energy to help meet this goal and their energy needs. Be sure to discuss matters of concern regarding energy use, such as cost and environmental impact, and make comparisons among various energy sources regarding these. Include statistics from a variety of sources to help support your position.

Possible positions:

- Nuclear energy should be completely relied on.
- Nuclear energy should be mostly relied on.
- Nuclear energy should be partially relied on.
- Nuclear energy should be slightly relied on.
- Nuclear energy should not be relied on.

Part

4 Planning the essay

Section 1 Writing a thesis

After doing research and taking a position, the next stage in preparing to write is to create an outline. An outline helps:

- organize ideas in a way that most effectively supports the writer's position.
- guarantee that the writer stays focused when writing the essay.

The first step in creating an outline is writing the thesis. A thesis is a sentence which states the writer's position on a topic. It is the most important sentence in the essay because it tells readers the purpose of the essay.

An effective thesis should include:

- the topic of the essay.
- the writer's position on the topic.

For the essay prompt:

Analyze the growth of Apple's market share since the introduction of the iMac.

a thesis may be:

The rapid growth of Apple's market share since the introduction of the iMac was due to a number of innovations in design, manufacturing, and marketing.

A breakdown of this thesis shows it has the necessary components:

Topic

The rapid growth of Apple's market share since the introduction of the iMac was due to a number of innovations in design, manufacturing, and marketing.

Position

For the longer essay prompt:

Many governments, for a variety of reasons, are seeking energy sources which can help them curb their reliance on fossil fuels. Assess how much countries should rely on nuclear energy to help meet this goal and their energy needs. Be sure to discuss matters of concern regarding energy use, such as cost and environmental impact, and make comparisons among various energy sources regarding these. Include statistics from a variety of sources to help support your position.

a thesis may be:

Topic ↓ *nuclear energy*; Position ↓ *still seems to be the only option …*

Despite fears over its safety, nuclear energy still seems to be the only option to sufficiently meet the demands of an increasingly energy-hungry world while limiting damage to the environment.

This is an effective thesis because it contains the topic and the writer's position.

Directly responding to the essay prompt

It is also important to ensure that the thesis directly responds to the essay prompt. The following examples are not suitable because they do not do so.

For the prompt:

Analyze the growth of Apple's market share since the introduction of the iMac.

a thesis such as:

✗ *Apple's rapid growth since the introduction of the iMac shows why it produces some of the best products in the world.*

is *not* suitable because:

- it does not indicate that there is any analysis of the reasons for Apple's growth.
- it gives an evaluation when the prompt only asked for an analysis.

For the prompt:

Many governments, for a variety of reasons, are seeking energy sources which can help them curb their reliance on fossil fuels. Assess how much countries should rely on nuclear energy to help meet this goal and their energy needs. Be sure to discuss matters of concern regarding energy use, such as cost and environmental impact, and make comparisons among various energy sources regarding these. Include statistics from a variety of sources to help support your position.

a thesis such as:

✗ *To eliminate the use of nuclear energy, people around the world should stop consuming too much energy, and families should not have more than one child.*

is *not* suitable because it is off-topic. This thesis offers recommendations for people around the world rather than an assessment of how much countries should rely on nuclear energy.

Exercise 1

For each essay prompt below, choose the thesis which comes closest to satisfactorily replying to the prompt.

1. Describe the American judicial system and how it is designed to limit wrongful convictions.
   a. The American judicial system is better than most in the world because it limits wrongful convictions.
   b. The American judicial system eliminates wrongful convictions.
   c. The American judicial system has several aspects which are meant to try to prevent wrongful convictions.

2. Watch the movie *Mulholland Drive* and identify its "film noir" characteristics. Refer to the aspects of the classic movies from the 1950s covered in the lecture.
   a. *Mulholland Drive* was a failure at the box office because of its "film noir" characteristics.
   b. *Mulholland Drive* is somewhat similar to "film noir" of the 1950s both visually and in its storyline.
   c. *Mulholland Drive* is a more modern but confusing version of classic "film noir."

3. Using points from the various readings assigned this semester, determine the most critical turning points in the evolution of human societies.

   a. Human societies have evolved a great deal over a long period of time.

   b. Human societies have evolved to the point where people are able to live longer lives now than ever before.

   c. Human societies seem to have undergone the most significant changes after the introduction of certain revolutionary technology.

4. The lectures in this course have thus far focused on the 30 articles in the U.N. Declaration of Human Rights and the historical basis for each. Select one of the Declaration's member countries and describe the challenges it faces in trying to uphold the human rights standards outlined in the articles. Determine how close the country is to being a model human rights state.

   a. Sweden is the best country in the world because it perfectly meets all of the U.N.'s standards for human rights.

   b. No country is a model human rights state because every one of them has faults in their treatment of people.

   c. The United States falls short of meeting a number of the U.N.'s standards for human rights.

Section 2 Making an outline

When creating an outline, include:

- the thesis statement (full sentence).
- the main arguments supporting the thesis (full sentences).
- the supporting points under each main argument (bullet points).

An outline for an essay is often structured as follows:

OUTLINE

Thesis:

Main argument 1

- **Supporting point 1**
- **Supporting point 2**
- **Supporting point …**

Main argument 2

- **Supporting point 1**
- **Supporting point 2**
- **Supporting point …**

Main argument 3

- **Supporting point 1**
- **Supporting point 2**
- **Supporting point …**

Main argument …

Exercise 2

For the essay prompt:

> Many governments, for a variety of reasons, are seeking energy sources which can help them curb their reliance on fossil fuels. Assess how much countries should rely on nuclear energy to help meet this goal and their energy needs. Be sure to discuss matters of concern regarding energy use, such as cost and environmental impact, and make comparisons among various energy sources regarding these. Include statistics from a variety of sources to help support your position.

a possible thesis is:

Despite fears over its safety, nuclear energy still seems to be the only option to sufficiently meet the demands of an increasingly energy-hungry world while limiting damage to the environment.

Based on the research on page 13, below are some supporting points the writer could present in the essay. In the outline on the next page, place each of the supporting points under the main argument it supports.

- cheaper than natural gas and oil
- some think not safe, but unreasonable; other energy more deaths
- building nuclear power plants is expensive, but over time still cheaper
- production of nuclear energy is constant
- emits low CO_2
- nuclear energy – reliability of suppliers
- renewable energy – innovation still needed to make cheaper and more available
- renewable energy has potential, but not enough; erratic supply
- any energy source is expensive

OUTLINE

Thesis:

Despite fears over its safety, nuclear energy still seems to be the only option to sufficiently meet the demands of an increasingly energy-hungry world while limiting damage to the environment.

Main argument 1

One benefit of nuclear power is that it is a much cleaner and safer energy source than fossil fuels.

Supporting points:

•

•

•

Main argument 2

Another appeal of nuclear power is that the cost of production is extremely low for such an efficient energy source.

Supporting points:

•

•

•

Main argument 3

Another reason nuclear power should be a significant part of the world's energy supply is its reliability.

Supporting points:

•

•

•

Read the the essay prompt and the following model essay.

Many governments, for a variety of reasons, are seeking energy sources which can help them curb their reliance on fossil fuels. Assess how much countries should rely on nuclear energy to help meet this goal and their energy needs. Be sure to discuss matters of concern regarding energy use, such as cost and environmental impact, and make comparisons among various energy sources regarding these. Include statistics from a variety of sources to help support your position.

NUCLEAR POWER:
A viable means of meeting our future energy demands

One way to measure a country's economic and social development is its increased usage of and reliance on energy. Most people now heat or cool their homes, cook, wash, power their TV or computer, and commute using energy mostly derived from fossil fuels. Our ancestors who lived as recently as 100 years ago would marvel at how much energy is used now and taken for granted. However, as the world's population has surpassed seven billion, and a growing proportion are seeing big increases in their wealth and energy consumption, achieving energy sufficiency while minimizing environmental damage is a challenging but crucial task. Undoubtedly, the key to environmental sustainability is curbing the overuse of and dependency on environmentally damaging fossil fuels like coal, natural gas, and oil. Many believe that increasing the reliance on nuclear power – a relatively clean, cheap, and reliable form of energy – is the answer. It contributes a vital 13.4% of the world's energy supply (International Energy Agency, 2011), and in Asia, a region where nuclear energy is in favor (Chang & Thomson, 2011), 301 new reactors are either under construction, planned, or proposed (World Nuclear Association, 2010). Others, wary of the potential risks of nuclear power, see a solution in harnessing the power available through natural sources such as wind or sunlight. Yet, while such renewable forms of energy have incredible potential and have recently seen increased investment and innovation, none of them have been shown to be able to produce energy on a level anywhere close to that currently being consumed around the world. Therefore, at least for the time being, despite fears over its safety, nuclear energy seems to be the only viable option for satisfying the demands of an increasingly energy-hungry world while limiting damage to the environment.

One benefit of nuclear power is that it is a much cleaner and safer energy source than fossil fuels. Nuclear energy emits virtually no environmentally harmful carbon. British Energy (2005) asserts that the total CO_2 emissions from the Torness nuclear reactor in Scotland are estimated to be just over 5 grams per kilowatt hour (g/kWh), compared to the 900 g/kWh produced by a coal plant (p. 6). Indeed, research by the International Energy Agency (2011) showed that greenhouse gas emissions over a nuclear reactor's lifecycle are actually lower than what wind or solar power would emit over a similar period at a similar wattage. It is apparent then that nuclear energy has a crucial part to play in lowering the world's carbon emissions and safeguarding the environment. Its critics, however, question whether nuclear energy is especially clean, given the necessity of storing radioactive waste nuclear power produces, and the potential release of harmful levels of radiation through nuclear accidents. The Chernobyl accident in 1986 led to 31 fatalities, and subsequently many more radiation-related deaths (Nuclear Energy Institute, 2011). The environmental and human cost of the nuclear leaks in 2011 from a reactor in Fukushima, Japan, after it was hit by a tsunami, is still being quantified. Incidents such as these ignite fears over nuclear safety, leading to fierce resistance by the public in certain countries towards building new reactors. For many, the risks of increasing the use of nuclear power outweigh any advantages. However, it seems unreasonable to equate these two disasters with nuclear plants everywhere. By far, the vast majority of the world's nuclear plants are not at risk from a tsunami, and the rigorous prevention, monitoring, and containment procedures in reactors now virtually eliminate the likelihood of another Chernobyl-like accident (Nuclear Energy Institute, 2011). It is also a mistake to believe other energy sources are entirely safe. Between 1969 and 2000, fatalities from coal extraction numbered over 20,000, and hydropower generation accounted for approximately 30,000 deaths, dwarfing the number of fatalities from nuclear disasters (Nuclear Energy Agency, 2010). In addition to public concerns about dangerous emissions, worries have also been expressed over what happens with waste from plants.

The fear over nuclear waste is commonly misunderstood. According to Cambridge University physics professor David MacKay (2008), nuclear power produces about 760 ml of radioactive waste per person, per year, that must be securely stored for about 1,000 years. Of this amount, however, only about 25 ml is actually dangerous. This amount is minute compared to the other wastes humans produce each year, including 517 kgs of garbage, and 83 kgs of hazardous industrial waste per person. Correspondingly, the amount of land required to store garbage and dangerous toxic waste is much larger and, due to its threats to both the environment and human health, much of the waste must be securely isolated from its surroundings. Given that society already tolerates having to deal with such a massive amount of hazardous waste, exercising similar precautions for equally dangerous but far less abundant nuclear waste does not seem to warrant special concern. Hopefully, careful consideration of these facts will lead the general public to recognize nuclear power's advantages in terms of cleanliness and safety. Indeed, it should be a significant part of any country's plans to reduce its dependence on fossil fuels.

Another appeal of nuclear power is that the cost of production is extremely low for such an efficient energy source. With energy demands increasing, producing enough energy is vital, and keeping costs low is necessary for making sure energy remains affordable. The U.N. Secretary-General, Bani Ki-Moon, in addressing the world's growing population, has consistently emphasized the necessity of supplying the poor with cheap electricity (United Nations Population Fund, 2011) – and few forms of electricity come cheaper than nuclear energy. Nuclear energy can be produced at 2.14 cents per kilowatt hour (kWh), compared with natural gas (4.86 cents per kWh), and oil (15.18 cents per kWh) (Nuclear Energy Institute, 2010). Essentially, the many parts of the world eager to become less reliant on fossil fuels are unlikely to find a more cost-effective alternative to nuclear energy. However, many claim that the expense of building nuclear power plants makes nuclear energy far more expensive than one might assume for the cost of energy generation. The huge cost of planning, designing, and funding nuclear power plants, critics assert, as well as the length of time required to achieve fully functioning power plants (given how politically fraught the issue is), means nuclear energy is a prohibitively expensive enterprise. A proposed nuclear reactor in Britain is estimated to cost $7.9 billion (Nuclear power: Nukes of hazard, 2011), which is a massive outlay at a time when government budgets are stretched. But as Kimura (2011) stresses, although the initial expense of nuclear power is extremely high, once the plants are functioning, this cost is not so significant when divided by the years the station will be generating electricity. In contrast, *The Economist* notes that solar power use remains largely confined to individuals who can afford the expensive solar panels, or to companies able to buy the many expensive panels and the large amount of land required to create solar farms (Solar power, 2011). It is hoped that as solar power costs fall, and its ability to generate sufficient electricity increases, its acceptance and adoption at the local level will increase greatly (Roaf & Gupta, 2007; MacKay, 2008). Yet, as development of the technology is slow and incremental, this seems a long way off. Radical breakthroughs are necessary to make renewable energy as widely available and cheap as nuclear power is now. Therefore, while renewable energy has undeniable promise, nuclear energy remains the most viable, available energy source for a world with an ever-increasing appetite for energy.

A further reason why nuclear power should be a significant part of the world's energy supply is its reliability. Once nuclear power plants are built and functioning, the production of nuclear energy is constant. Wind and solar power, however, are intermittent energy producers. Wind turbines are not much use when there is no wind, while solar power has limited potential in, say, cloud-covered Northern Europe. A key advantage of nuclear power is that, come gale, rain or shine, nuclear energy is still generated. Nuclear power plants can also depend on having a stable supply of materials. Oil and gas are currently produced in relatively unstable regions of the world, which makes an over-reliance on this energy source risky to the extent that it could jeopardize national security. Accordingly, as Moran and Russell (2009) point out, issues of energy security are now high on the agendas of political leaders throughout the world. In contrast, the primary source of nuclear power – uranium – is easily supplied by Canada and Australia, two comparatively stable countries (Nuclear power: Nukes of hazard, 2011). With the regular supply of uranium guaranteed, nuclear energy can be generated domestically at constant levels, forming the basis of a country's security and self-reliance. Many argue, though, that certain renewable energy forms that safely harness the earth's natural energy could become more reliable. Wind power is proving to be a growing, domestically generated, energy source. Solar power is even more promising: one hour of the sun's power contains more than humanity's energy needs for one year (Solar power, 2011). With increasing technical advances, its supporters claim, solar power can be responsible for a much greater share of energy production (Tanaka, 2010). However, despite the clear potential of such forms of energy, if nuclear energy generation were to cease immediately, renewable sources, given their current erratic nature, would be unable to meet the 13.4% required to make up the deficit. As the world tries to gradually move away from its reliance on fossil fuels, nuclear power still remains the only energy supply constant enough to depend on for an adequate supply of energy.

It is apparent that nuclear power does offer a realistic means of meeting the world's growing energy demands, while at the same time limiting environmental destruction. Nuclear energy is clean and cheap, its production is reliable, and its materials are readily available. However, as a result of several major nuclear accidents, the public is wary of potential disasters on their doorstep, making nuclear power a currently unpopular choice. On the other hand, renewable energy, which is far more accepted and much easier to champion, remains unable to provide a significant share the world's energy needs. Perhaps in the future the huge potential of solar, wind, or some other form of renewable energy will be unlocked, allowing it to power all that fossil fuels power now. Until then, governments and the nuclear energy industry should make the case for nuclear energy more aggressively to appease a nervous but seemingly misinformed public about the role nuclear power plays in making life comfortable for so many around the world.

References

British Energy. (2005, May). Environmental product declaration of electricity from Torness Nuclear Power Station summary of results. Retrieved from http://www.britishenergy.com/documents/EPD_Exec_Summary.pdf

Chang, Y., & Thomson, E. (2011). East Asian energy supply, demand and cooperation outlook. In E. Thomson, Y. Chang, & J. S. Lee (Eds.), *Energy conservation in East Asia: Towards greater energy security.* Singapore: World Scientific Publishing Co. Pte. Ltd.

International Energy Agency. (2011). Key world energy statistics. Retrieved from http://www.iea.org/textbase/nppdf/free/2011/key_world_energy_stats.pdf

Kimura, I. (2011). 核エネルギーと世論 — 核保有の恐怖と非核の恐怖 [*Nuclear energy and public opinion – Fear with it, fear without it*]. Tokyo: Narimasu Press.

MacKay, D. J. C. (2008, November 3). Sustainable energy – Without the hot air. Retrieved from http://www.inference.phy.cam.ac.uk/sustainable/book/tex/sewtha.pdf

Moran, D., & Russell, J. A. (Eds.). (2009). *Energy security and global politics: The militarization of resource management.* London: Routledge.

Nuclear Energy Agency. (2010). Comparing nuclear accident risks with those from other resources. Retrieved from http://www.oecd-nea.org/ndd/reports/2010/nea6861-comparing-risks.pdf

Nuclear Energy Institute. (2010). Economic growth. Retrieved from http://www.nei.org/keyissues/reliableandaffordableenergy/economicgrowth/

Nuclear Energy Institute. (2011, July). Chernobyl accident and its consequences. Retrieved from http://www.nei.org/filefolder/Chernobyl_Accident_and_Its_Consequences_July_2011_4

Nuclear power: Nukes of hazard. (2011, October 15). *The Economist.* Retrieved from htttp://www.economist.com/node/21532330

Roaf, S., & Gupta, R. (2007). Solar power: Using energy from the sun in buildings. In D. Elliot (Ed.), *Sustainable energy: opportunities and limitations* (pp. 84–107). Basingstoke, England: Palgrave Macmillan.

Solar power: A painful eclipse. (2011, October 15). *The Economist.* Retrieved from http://www.economist.com/node/21532279

Tanaka, N. (2010, May). Solar for the energy revolution: IEA launches the PV and CSP roadmaps [PowerPoint slides with speech transcript in PDF document]. Retrieved from http://www.iea.org/speechia_notes.pdf

United Nations Population Fund. (2011, October 26). State of world population 2011. Retrieved from http://foweb.unfpa.org/SWP2011/reports/EN-SWOP2011-FINAL.pdf

World Nuclear Association. (2010, April). Asia's nuclear energy growth. Retrieved from http://world-nuclear.org/info/inf47.html

Exercise 3

Here is the essay prompt for the model essay again with each of the instructional words numbered (1–4):

2 1

> Many governments, for a variety of reasons, are seeking energy sources which can help them curb their reliance on fossil fuels. Assess (1) how much countries should rely on nuclear energy to help meet this goal and their energy needs. Be sure to discuss (2) matters of concern regarding energy use, such as cost and environmental impact, and make comparisons (3) among various energy sources regarding these. Include (4) statistics from a variety of sources to help support your position.

4 3

Go through the model essay and label each part of the essay that answers these four instructions with the appropriate number. For example:

> 3 … Others, wary of the potential risks of nuclear power, see a solution in harnessing the power available through natural sources such as wind or sunlight. Yet, while such renewable forms of energy have incredible potential and have recently seen increased investment and innovation, none of them have been shown to be able to produce energy on a level anywhere close to that currently being consumed around the world. 1 Therefore, at least for the time being, despite fears over its safety, nuclear energy seems to be the only viable option for satisfying the demands of an increasingly energy-hungry world while limiting damage to the environment.
>
> 2 One benefit of nuclear power is that it is a much cleaner and safer energy source than fossil fuels. Nuclear energy emits virtually no environmentally harmful carbon. 4 British Energy (2005) asserts that the total CO_2 emissions from the Torness nuclear reactor in Scotland are estimated to be just over 5 grams per kilowatt hour (g/kWh), compared to the 900 g/kWh produced by a coal plant (p. 6). Indeed, research, …

UNIT

2

Essay Paragraphs

Part 1

Introductory paragraphs

The introductory paragraph should introduce the essay topic and prepare readers for the contents of the essay. Therefore, there are certain things writers should consider when making decisions about any introductory paragraph.

The introductory paragraph can be written **before** or **after** the rest of the essay. Writing it before the rest of the essay follows a logical order, as it is the first paragraph of the essay, and it also helps to focus the writer on the specific contents of the essay. When the essay is finished, the writer can revise the introductory paragraph written at the start to ensure its contents match the essay. However, if writers do not have fully formed ideas about all the contents of the essay, they may waste time deciding what to write in the introductory paragraph.

Therefore:

- write the introductory paragraph without worrying about perfection.

OR

- write the introductory paragraph after writing the body paragraphs.

Section 1 What to include

What to include in an introductory paragraph depends on the topic, the type of essay being written, and the target reader. However, in general, the introductory paragraph should consist of three parts:

1. background on the topic.
2. the writer's thesis.
3. a motive for the essay.

1. Background on the topic

Suitable background is information such as:

- a history of the topic.
- the current situation regarding the topic.
- different perspectives on the topic.
- definitions of key terms.
- statistics.

The following introductory paragraph includes all these features.

Statistics

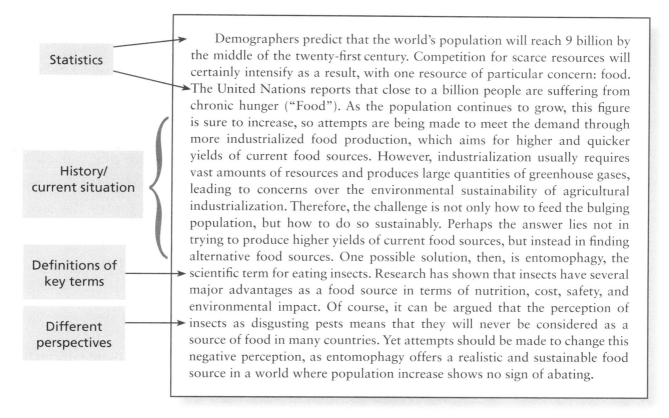

History/ current situation

Definitions of key terms

Different perspectives

> Demographers predict that the world's population will reach 9 billion by the middle of the twenty-first century. Competition for scarce resources will certainly intensify as a result, with one resource of particular concern: food. The United Nations reports that close to a billion people are suffering from chronic hunger ("Food"). As the population continues to grow, this figure is sure to increase, so attempts are being made to meet the demand through more industrialized food production, which aims for higher and quicker yields of current food sources. However, industrialization usually requires vast amounts of resources and produces large quantities of greenhouse gases, leading to concerns over the environmental sustainability of agricultural industrialization. Therefore, the challenge is not only how to feed the bulging population, but how to do so sustainably. Perhaps the answer lies not in trying to produce higher yields of current food sources, but instead in finding alternative food sources. One possible solution, then, is entomophagy, the scientific term for eating insects. Research has shown that insects have several major advantages as a food source in terms of nutrition, cost, safety, and environmental impact. Of course, it can be argued that the perception of insects as disgusting pests means that they will never be considered as a source of food in many countries. Yet attempts should be made to change this negative perception, as entomophagy offers a realistic and sustainable food source in a world where population increase shows no sign of abating.

Exercise 1

Look at the introductory paragraph of the model essay on page 24. Label the different parts of the introductory paragraph (follow the example above).

Selecting background to include

Background information depends on the essay topic. The key question is:

What background information is necessary for readers to understand the essay contents?

If the essay topic is familiar, provide a brief background and focus on presenting information which may challenge what readers already believe about the topic. For example:

Topic: Causes in the rise in worldwide obesity

Thesis: *The rise in worldwide obesity rates has less to do with the spread of American-style fast food, and has more to do with an increase in the American-style "fast life."*

Readers may be familiar with this issue and have assumptions about its causes. Appropriate background could be:

- statistics on the rise in worldwide obesity.
- clarification of how many kilograms overweight is considered obese.
- previous assumptions about the causes of obesity, plus a challenge to that assumption:

Assumption → *Although many people blame "fast-food culture" for the rise of obesity in many parts of the world, new research has revealed that fast-food meals have no more calories than home-cooked ones.* ← Challenge

If the topic is less familiar, more background information may be necessary for the reader to understand the topic. For example:

Topic: Ways to improve the lives of people in developing countries

Thesis: *Funding for desalination plants is one way to increase social stability and economic growth in those areas of the developing world in need of fresh water, a resource arguably more vital than oil and more precious than gold.*

Readers may be unfamiliar with two key parts of the thesis – the issue of water shortage and desalination plants. Appropriate background could be:

- the scope of the water shortage problem (e.g., countries affected, how lives are affected, resulting social and economic problems).
- statistics on water availability.
- a definition and description of "desalination."

Exercise 2

For each thesis statement below, list appropriate background information to help readers understand the essay topic.

1. **Thesis:** Arranged marriages are still an integral aspect of many cultures and actually seem to be more stable than the more modern "love marriages."

   Background:

   ____

   ____

   ____

   ____

   ____

2. **Thesis:** Although people are better informed about other cultures through the internet, racism and ethnocentrism is apparently increasing, as people find more opportunities to compare their own culture to that of others.

   Background:

   ____

   ____

   ____

   ____

   ____

3. **Thesis:** The argument could be made that nanotechnology has been the most influential science in the twenty-first century, due to the number of life-changing products developed from it.

Background:

____

____

____

____

____

4. **Thesis:** An analysis of the bodily features of the main actors in the top 25 highest grossing movies of today versus those 30 years ago indicates some similarities and differences in what is considered physically attractive in males and females.

Background:

____

____

____

____

____

5. **Thesis:** The vast sums of money spent trying to deter drug trafficking and drug abuse seem to have had little or no effect, thereby warranting the implementation of more radical tactics in the "war on drugs."

Background:

____

____

____

____

____

2. The writer's thesis

As explained in Unit 1, the thesis is a clear statement of the writer's position on the topic. It is often the last sentence of the introductory paragraph.

In the sample paragraph on entomophagy (page 33), the thesis is the last sentence:

Yet attempts should be made to change this negative perception, as entomophagy offers a realistic and sustainable food source in a world where population increase shows no sign of abating.

Everything that follows in the essay should focus on showing how and why this thesis is valid.

3. A motive for the essay

While the thesis is the writer's position on the topic, the motive is the reason why it is necessary to take this position or why the topic is worth exploring. The motive explains to the reader the situation which led to the thesis. A common indicator of a motive is by the use of the words *but*, *however*, or *although*.

The following are three common motives for an academic essay:

❶ There is an issue worthy of debate.

a. **Thesis:** *The internet has made society less efficient, less informed, and less healthy.*

Motive: *Some view the internet as an overwhelmingly positive force which has benefited mankind.*

b. **Thesis:** *The concepts of marriage and monogamy evolved from societal necessities, rather than innate human tendencies.*

Motive: *It is widely accepted that finding a life partner in marriage and having children is a natural goal for humans. However, research has cast doubt on whether or not marriage can be considered natural.*

❷ There is a problem requiring a solution or explanation.

a. **Thesis:** *To lower recidivism rates among violent criminals who return to society, the time they spend in prison should focus on keeping their mind and body active with productive activities that foster ambition and self-confidence.*

Motive: *For most countries, prison is the main means for punishing criminal behavior and making society safer. However, while prison does protect society in the short-term by keeping criminals away from ordinary citizens, incarceration and lengthy prison sentences seem to be counter-effective in reducing violent crime rates in the long-term.*

b. **Thesis:** *The paradox of increased IT spending by companies but lower productivity and increased work hours is attributable to a number of factors related to employer expectations, difficulties in measuring productivity, and significant shortcomings in computer-based work.*

Motive: *The spread of computers should have signaled the dawn of an era of efficiency in the workplace, leading to increased productivity and shorter work hours. However, statistics show that productivity has dropped and work hours have increased since computers became ubiquitous in offices all around the developed world.*

❸ There is information which may aid understanding.

a. **Thesis:** *It is clear that students in families living in poverty have few of the types of social and parental interactions necessary to properly prepare them for the challenges of academic study.*

Motive: *It is well documented that students from impoverished backgrounds tend to perform poorly in school compared with their more affluent counterparts. However, while reducing the cost of education does alleviate some of the financial burden, research has indicated that certain factors common in these students' lives outside school have a greater influence on their poor academic performance.*

b. **Thesis:** *A major reason why Western celebrities are popular in Asia but Asian celebrities are less so in the West is that the Western cultural products have vastly superior financial and marketing strength.*

Motive: *Western athletes, actors, and singers enjoy huge followings all around Asia. However, attempts by their Asian counterparts to create similar levels of popularity in the West have met with minimal success. Part of understanding the appeal of Western celebrities in Asia requires an examination of the relative power of their cultural industries.*

Exercise 3

Look at the introductory paragraph of the model essay on page 24.

1. **Underline the motive.**

2. **Decide which type of motivating point it is, and write the number in the margin next to the motive.**

Exercise 4

For introductory paragraphs a, b, and c below:

1. **Underline the motive.**

2. **Decide which type of motivating point it is, and write the number in the margin next to the motive.**

Example:

Nowhere else in the world do Emperor penguins live, do 4,000 meter-deep ice sheets exist, do distant galaxies shine brighter, or do winds blow colder. The extreme climate of the Antarctic and its remote location on the globe make it an ideal laboratory. Scientific research of such rare conditions may offer the potential to better understand the entire global ecosystem. Because of the efforts of scientists and documentarians, who bring back rare data and footage informing the public about Antarctica's features and ecosystem, the interest among tourists to see and experience this unspoiled place has grown exponentially. ❷ **Many laud the once-in-a-lifetime trip to Antarctica as experiential education in eco-tourism, a category of traveling focused on environmental conservation and minimal invasiveness on a natural area. Tourism dollars are also a valuable potential source of funds to help finance the many ongoing scientific experiments being conducted. However, despite these benefits, the presence of humans in Antarctica, particularly that of tourists, has been unavoidably intrusive.** The sheer number of visitors has resulted in unprecedented damage to the continent, with scientists warning that, unless significant measures are taken, the increasing number of tourists will inevitably bring irreparable future disruptions to the fragile ecosystem there, with possible ripple effects around the world. As Antarctica has no government or rule of law to protect itself, the onus is on scientists, governments, and tour operators to coordinate their efforts to ensure visitors maximize their travel experience without negatively impacting Antarctica's environment.

a. Much has been written about the cultural basis of seniority-based versus merit-based promotion and pay in companies, as well as the benefits and drawbacks of each system. A seniority-based system is more common in the East – e.g., Thailand, Japan – where the hard work and loyalty of company employees are rewarded with increased status and pay as they get older. While such a system virtually guarantees lifetime employment for employees, it also often breeds inefficiency and even laziness among those who feel there is no incentive to do more than what is required of their position. A merit-based system, however, is prevalent in the West – e.g., the United States, the U.K. – where productivity is the basis of position and pay. It gives employees the incentive to work hard and be innovative, but it also often leads to competition among employees, resulting in distrust and conflict in the workplace as well as less job security. Studies have indicated that there seems to be a shift toward a more merit-based system among companies in the East, but a number of factors can help determine if such a shift is necessary or desirable.

b. Since the middle of the twentieth century, Keynesian economic theory has been the mainstay of governmental policies in regulating the economy. The theory essentially contends that in times of recession, a free-market economy may not be able to self-correct naturally, thereby requiring the government to intervene by trying to stimulate the economy with such measures as tax and interest rate cuts and increases in spending on various projects. Although Keynesian policy has been successful in the sense that there has not yet been a repeat of the Great Depression of 1929, the lingering effects of the market collapse of 2007–8 and subsequent recessions have shown that traditional government interventions are having relatively little effect in turning economies around. An explanation for this lies in examining particular aspects of modern communication, especially with regard to the effect of the media and "bandwagon" behavior.

c. Much credit is given to Hollywood for spreading American culture around the world through movies and TV shows. However, one might argue that another American export has had an equally or even more pervasive effect in capturing the minds and souls of people worldwide: hip-hop. Hip-hop culture began on the streets of New York in the 1970s, as house and street parties in black and Hispanic communities provided a venue for listening to rap music and wearing loose-fitting brand sportswear as a fashion statement. Since then, hip-hop has won fans around the world, as youths have adopted its musical, clothing, and speaking styles, while also combining elements of their own culture. There are a number of factors which have driven hip-hop's popularity and helped create one of the world's truly global music styles.

Exercise 5

For each thesis below, write a possible motive.

a. **Thesis:** Witness testimony in criminal trials can be considered unreliable due to a number of factors which affect the ability of humans to accurately recall something or someone.

Motive: ____________________

____

____

____

____

____

b. **Thesis:** Developments in traffic management suggest the key to reducing accidents may be to reduce the number of instructions given to drivers through road signs.

Motive: ______________________________

____

____

____

____

____

c. **Thesis:** Despite being costly to host, the Olympics seem to bring a number of beneficial social effects for the host country.

Motive: ______________________________

____

____

____

____

____

d. **Thesis:** Traditional styles of medicine have a role to play alongside modern medical techniques.

Motive: ______________________________

____

____

____

____

____

e. **Thesis:** More focus should be placed on preventing health problems rather than dealing with them once they have already occurred.

Motive: ______________________________

____

____

____

____

____

Part

2 Body paragraphs

Purpose and parts

Essays are organized into a logical flow of information which demonstrates why the thesis is valid.

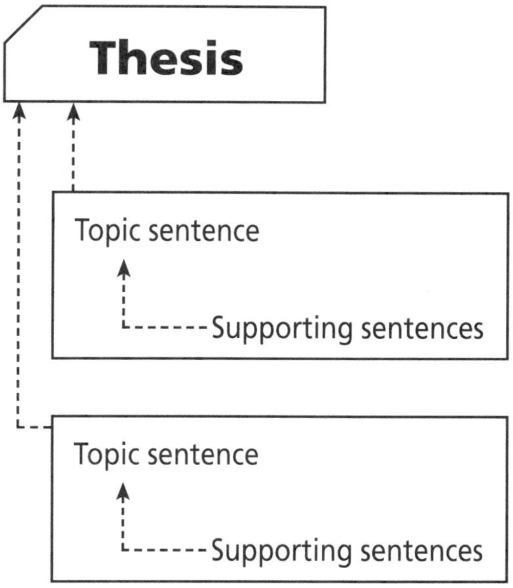

Body paragraphs follow the introduction. They form the majority of the essay because they present all the details supporting the thesis.

A body paragraph contains:

1. **A topic sentence**. This is usually the first sentence of a body paragraph. It states the topic and a controlling idea of that paragraph.
2. **Supporting sentences.** These are claims, evidence, and explanations which show how the controlling idea supports the essay's thesis.
3. An optional **transitional sentence**. This sentence can be at the end or beginning of a paragraph to indicate one idea is complete and a new one is beginning.

Topic sentences

Each body paragraph requires a clear topic sentence, which states what the body paragraph will be about. The sentence includes:

- the topic – the theme of the paragraph which is related to the thesis.
- a controlling idea – the specific focus of the paragraph. All the details in the body paragraph support the controlling idea.

Here is a thesis and topic sentence from an essay on photography's influence on art:

Thesis: *Photography dramatically influenced artists by a affecting their subject matter, level of detail, and development of new styles.*

Topic sentence:
One effect photography had on artists was in changing the subjects in their paintings.

Topic — Controlling idea

The above topic sentence shows that the paragraph will be:

- linked to the thesis about the "effect photography had on artists."
- specifically about how photography was influential in "changing the subjects in their paintings."

Topic sentences

- can begin with either the topic or controlling idea.
- should use precise words for stating the topic and controlling idea, avoiding pronouns such as *they*, *it*, or *these*, or words such as *reason*, *aspect*, or *effect* when they are not clearly explained.

Examples:

✗ *It was also a new creative medium for artists.*
✗ *Creating a new medium for artists was also an effect.*

These two topic sentences are ineffective because they do not give readers a clear idea of what the paragraph will be about, nor do they remind readers what the thesis of the essay is.

✓ *Photography also inspired artists to explore a new medium by which art could be created.*

This topic sentence is effective because it is clear that the essay is about how photography affected artists and that the controlling idea of the paragraph will be about how artists began using photography as a medium to produce art.

Exercise 1

Read the following topic sentences. Circle the topic and underline the controlling idea if possible. Decide the effectiveness of each topic sentence.

1. As of 2008, over half of the people using a social networking service were over 35 years old.

2. First, cars are safer today than ever before because airbags have become a standard safety feature.

3. Furthermore, although not an old technology, they have already become obsolete.

4. Increased productivity in the workplace has been another result of staff being allowed to use their own tablet computers.

5. Another limitation is that electricity cannot be generated at night.

Relevance

When writing a topic sentence, it is important that the topic sentence shows its relevance to the essay thesis. Here is a thesis and two topic sentences:

Certain aspects of reality TV shows reflect the American character and preferences which enable these programs to dominate television ratings in the U.S.

a. *One reason there are so many reality TV shows is that they are relatively inexpensive to produce.*
b. *Through reality TV, American society has shown a voyeuristic desire to look into the lives of other, "ordinary" people.*

Topic sentence "**a**" is irrelevant because, although it is about reality TV shows, it is not related to the idea of how it reflects the American character. Topic sentence "**b**" is relevant because it mentions a specific character trait: being voyeuristic.

Exercise 2

For each thesis on the next page, read each topic sentence and:

- circle the topic and underline the controlling idea.

- determine if the topic sentence logically supports the thesis by writing "yes" or "no" in the space next to it.

1. **Thesis:** *Certain aspects of reality TV shows reflect the American character and preferences which enable these programs to dominate television ratings in the U.S.*

Potential topic sentences:

a. Reality TV has also caught on in Asia, so much so that they have started their own shows there which are similar or even direct copies of the original American versions. ________________

b. Many of the participants in the most popular reality TV shows are there to achieve status and prestige, which is indicative of what motivates Americans in general in many aspects of their life. ________________

c. Almost every major TV network in the U.S. has its own lineup of reality TV shows, with new ones debuting every season. ________________

d. Reality TV also highlights the competitive nature of Americans, as many shows have features which make them as dramatic as sports events. ________________

2. **Thesis:** *With society's high value on personal and environmental health, an increasing number of people are becoming vegetarians because of the benefits it brings to individuals and the world's ecosystem.*

Potential topic sentences:

a. Adopting a vegetarian diet is widely believed to reduce the risk of many illnesses. ________________

b. Vegetarians used to be known as Pythagoreans, after the ancient Greek philosopher and mathematician Pythagoras, an early advocate of non-meat diets. ________________

c. A vegetarian lifestyle is also seen as fashionable among some young people. ________________

d. The success of animal rights groups over the last four decades has created a generation expecting the ethical treatment of animals. ________________

e. Adopting a vegetarian diet is also believed to contribute to a reduction in greenhouse gases that cause global warming. ________________

f. In many Western countries, Asian food has become much more popular due to its perceived health benefits. ________________

g. Another factor is protecting the balance of the world's ecosystem. ________________

Section 2 Supporting sentences and the "waltz"

Supporting sentences follow the topic sentence in a body paragraph. They provide details that support the controlling idea. To organize these sentences, use the paragraph "waltz." The waltz is a way to write supporting sentences so that they work together to logically develop ideas to support the controlling idea. The waltz has three parts:

Part 1	**A claim:**	a sentence or sentences introducing a specific point about the controlling idea. One or more claims may be introduced in a body paragraph.
Part 2	**Evidence:**	a sentence or sentences providing one or more examples, statistics, or other evidence supporting each claim.
Part 3	**An explanation:**	a sentence or sentences explaining the meaning of each claim and evidence, and showing their significance, relevance, or implication to the controlling idea.

Examples

a. **Part 1: Body paragraph developing one claim for the topic sentence on page 42.**

Topic sentence

Introducing the *claim*

One effect photography had on artists was in changing the subjects in their paintings. Prior to the camera, the subjects in paintings were often of religion, wealthy people, or landscapes. However, during the nineteenth century, photographs of ordinary people going about their everyday lives inspired artists to use these subjects in their paintings.

In this example, the controlling idea in the topic sentence is photography "changing the subjects in their paintings." The claim, "photographs of ordinary people going about their everyday lives inspired artists to use these subjects in their paintings," supports the controlling idea that photography changed the subjects in paintings. The essay writer needed to write two sentences to express this one claim clearly.

b. Part 2: Evidence added to support the claim

Introducing the *claim*

Evidence supporting the *claim*

> One effect photography had on artists was in changing the subjects in their paintings. Prior to the camera, the subjects in paintings were often of religion, wealthy people, or landscapes. However, during the nineteenth century, photographs of ordinary people going about their everyday lives inspired artists to use these subjects in their paintings. According to Biggs (2001), *The Umbrellas* by Pierre-Auguste Renoir, in which the artist depicts a rainy street scene in Paris, vividly exemplifies this influence. The people in the painting are not posing. The principal female figure and a young girl look out at the viewer as if they notice they are being watched while the other figures appear only concerned about making their way in the rain; one female figure is even shown in the act of raising her umbrella. Another figure, a man, is shown to be on the verge of speaking to the principal female figure, which suggests the painting is like a photograph of people on a typical rainy day.

In this example, the painting *The Umbrellas* is the evidence which shows that the claim "ordinary people going about their everyday lives" is true. The essay writer needed several sentences to describe this evidence clearly.

c. Part 3: Explanation added to express the significance of the claim and evidence

The explanation in the waltz is crucial to make the reader understand why or how the claim and evidence support the controlling idea and the thesis.

> One effect photography had on artists was in changing the subjects in their paintings. Prior to the camera, the subjects in paintings were often of religion, wealthy people, or landscapes. However, during the nineteenth century, photographs of ordinary people going about their everyday lives inspired artists to use these subjects in their paintings. According to Biggs (2001), *The Umbrellas* by Pierre-Auguste Renoir, in which the artist depicts a rainy street scene in Paris, vividly exemplifies this influence. The people in the painting are not posing. The principal female figure and a young girl look out at the viewer as if they notice they are being watched while the other figures appear only concerned about making their way in the rain; one female figure is even shown in the act of raising her umbrella. Another figure, a man, is shown to be on the verge of speaking to the principal female figure, which suggests the painting is like a photograph of people on a typical rainy day.

Explanation of the significance of the *claim* and *evidence*

> The result was a revolution in subject matter; the mundane events of life became interesting subjects, and elevated the common person to the status of worthy subject in serious art.

To be effective, the explanation should clearly express the meaning of the claim and evidence, and show their significance to the controlling idea. The explanation should not just repeat the claim or evidence. In this example, the meaning of the claim and evidence is: Photography caused a "revolution in subject matter" because photographs often had subjects of common people doing common things, as exemplified in *The Umbrellas*, so artists were inspired to also use these same, new subjects. Therefore, the writer concludes that "the mundane events of life became interesting subjects, and elevated the common person to the status of worthy subject in serious art."

d. Parts 2 and 3: Reversed position in a body paragraph

The order of the waltz parts can be changed. A claim usually follows the topic sentence to clearly establish the specific idea that will be developed. However, in the following waltz, the evidence and explanation are reversed.

Explanation of the significance of the *claim*

Evidence supporting the *claim* and *explanation*

> One effect photography had on artists was in changing the subjects in their paintings. Prior to the camera, the subjects in paintings were often of religion, wealthy people, or landscapes. However, during the nineteenth century, photographs of ordinary people going about their everyday lives inspired artists to use these subjects in their paintings. The result was a revolution in subject matter; the mundane events of life became interesting subjects, and elevated the common person to the status of worthy subject in serious art. According to Biggs (2001), *The Umbrellas* by Pierre-Auguste Renoir, in which the artist depicts a rainy street scene in Paris, vividly exemplifies this influence. The people in the painting are not posing. The principal female figure and a young girl look out at the viewer as if they notice they are being watched while the other figures appear only concerned about making their way in the rain; one female figure is even shown in the act of raising her umbrella. Another figure, a man, is shown to be on the verge of speaking to the principal female figure, which suggests the painting is like a photograph of people on a typical rainy day.

It is the writer's decision how to arrange the evidence and explanation parts in body paragraphs. In this example, the explanation is presented before the evidence. The writer may have decided that putting the explanation before the evidence was more effective in supporting the claim, or wanted to avoid repeating the same waltz organization in each body paragraph.

e. Body paragraphs with multiple claims

In a body paragraph with more than one claim, simply start a new waltz with the next claim.

Topic sentence	At the beginning of the twentieth century, the mass-production of cameras contributed to making society more equal.
1st *claim*	First, with George Eastman's development of photographic film in 1885, cameras became cheaper.
Evidence for 1st *claim*	For example, released in 1900, the Kodak Brownie was the world's first mass-produced camera. It sold for only $1 and became an immediate success with millions sold (McDougal, 2001).
Significance of 1st *claim* and *evidence*	The result of these inexpensive cameras was that photography became a new leisure activity accessible to all. People from all social classes could now afford to participate in an activity previously reserved for those with the free time and wealth needed to take pictures.
2nd *claim*	In addition, these cameras were easy to use and produced inexpensive photos, which led to the idea of the "snapshot."
Evidence for 2nd *claim*	Wilson (2003) describes snapshots as photos of everyday events such as birthday parties and other celebrations, animals, or travel destinations, characterized by their amateurish technique, spontaneity, and low picture quality.
Significance of 2nd *claim* and *evidence*	The ease of taking snapshots allowed everyone to record the unique events of their own lives.
Implications of 1st and 2nd *claim* and *evidence*	In short, mass-produced cameras played a role in equalizing society by allowing all social classes to pursue the same hobby, and by empowering ordinary people to visually express and document their own lives for the first time.

Exercise 3

Read the following thesis statement. Put the sentences for a body paragraph supporting this thesis into a logical order by numbering them 1–9.

Thesis: *Preventable diseases are a major cause of poverty in developing countries.*

Body paragraph sentences:

________ With no investment in infrastructure projects or business ventures, entire regions remain isolated and backwards because of the threat of malaria.

________ This impact on people results in a significant reduction in productivity and lost income, and inhibits daily commercial activity.

________ In all, malaria, a disease seen as a result of poverty, is also a significant contributor to poverty throughout the developing world.

________ First, communicable diseases such as malaria negatively affect the workforce.

________ The World Bank (2007) found that in areas where malaria outbreaks are commonly reported, investment from both domestic and international sources are virtually non-existent.

________ The presence of malaria also prevents larger scale economic development through discouraging investment.

________ Moreover, malaria prevents many people in developing regions who work from their homes from participating in the day-to-day commerce of their community.

________ The presence of disease limits the economic growth of many developing countries.

________ The World Health Organization (2010) estimates that malaria alone accounts for nearly 40 percent of absenteeism among workers in developing countries.

Exercise 4

Develop the ideas in the following body paragraphs.

1. Write an *explanation* in a body paragraph from an essay about the benefits of nuclear power.

Topic sentence	One of the main benefits of nuclear power is that it is relatively clean.
Claim	Nuclear power does not produce the same level of atmospheric pollution as fossil fuels.
Evidence	Burning fossil fuels produces 21 billion tons of carbon dioxide every year, and the planet can only absorb about half of that amount.
Explanation	

2. Write a *claim* and *explanation* for a body paragraph from an essay about making driving tests more difficult for older people:

Topic sentence	Another reason for making the driving test more difficult for older people is that it would likely increase road safety.
Claim	
Evidence	After about 60 years of age, people experience declines in reflexes, strength, eyesight, memory, concentration, and judgment as a result of the natural aging process.
Explanation	

Exercise 5

Write two logically organized and developed body paragraphs supporting the following thesis. Use the information provided to help write each paragraph.

Thesis: *Globalization is essentially Americanization, as U.S. culture has become a part of the daily lives of people in countries around the world.*

1. **Information:**

   McDonald's now operates over 25,000 restaurants worldwide, and opens six new ones per day.

Topic sentence	
Claim	
Evidence	
Explanation	

2. **Information:**

   About two-thirds of movie ticket sales around the world are for films made in the United States.

Topic sentence	
Claim	
Evidence	
Explanation	

Section 3 Transitional sentences

Transitional sentences can be placed at the end of a body paragraph, or at the beginning before the topic sentence. These sentences can be useful to:

- prepare the reader for a change in ideas.
- add emphasis to the new idea.

Here is an example of a transitional sentence placed at the end of a paragraph.

> One effect photography had on artists was in changing the subjects in their paintings. Prior to the camera, the subjects in paintings were often of religion, wealthy people, or landscapes. However, during the nineteenth century, photographs of ordinary people going about their everyday lives inspired artists to use these subjects in their paintings. According to Biggs (2001), *The Umbrellas* by Pierre-Auguste Renoir, in which the artist depicts a rainy street scene in Paris, vividly exemplifies this influence. The people in the painting are not posing. The principal female figure and a young girl look out at the viewer as if they notice they are being watched while the other figures appear only concerned about making their way in the rain; one female figure is even shown in the act of raising her umbrella. Another figure, a man, is shown to be on the verge of speaking to the principal female figure, which suggests the painting is like a photograph of people on a typical rainy day. The result was a revolution in subject matter; the mundane events of life became interesting subjects and elevated the common person to the status of worthy subject in serious art. Yet, photographs were perhaps more influential in prompting an even greater impact on art: detail.
>
> The camera also allowed painters to depict a greater level of detail previously not possible. Before photographs, …

Alternatively, the transitional sentence can be placed at the beginning of a paragraph:

> … The result was a revolution in subject matter; the mundane events of life became interesting subjects and elevated the common person to the status of worthy subject in serious art.
>
> Yet, photographs were perhaps more influential in prompting an even greater impact on art: detail. The camera allowed painters to depict a greater level of detail previously not possible. Before photographs, …

Section 4 Body paragraphs without topic sentences

Some body paragraphs have a controlling idea that requires many claims to support it. In these situations, it may be necessary to spread these claims over more than one paragraph. When more than one body paragraph develops the same controlling idea, only the first paragraph requires a complete topic sentence. The additional paragraphs can begin with a claim that supports the controlling idea from the previous paragraph.

In the essay in Exercise 6, body paragraph 6 has the topic sentence:

The Antarctic ecosystem is also threatened by environmental hazards brought by the increasing stream of tourists.

Body paragraph 7 continues to support the same controlling idea of *threatened by environmental hazards*, so it begins another waltz with another supporting claim:

Moreover, the threat of invasive microbes and other unseen organisms presents a major problem to the safety of the environment.

In the above claim, *invasive microbes and other unseen organisms* supports the controlling idea of *threatened by environmental hazards*.

Exercise 6

In the following essay:

1. Identify the topic and controlling idea in each body paragraph topic sentence.
2. Choose one body paragraph and identify the claim(s), evidence, and explanation parts of that paragraph.
3. Identify any transitional sentences in the essay.

Essay prompt:

The increase in tourism to Antarctica in recent decades has been a controversial issue. Outline the problems that tourism has created in the Antarctic region, and propose solutions that would address these problems.

Nowhere else in the world do Emperor penguins live, do 4,000 meter-deep ice sheets exist, do distant galaxies shine brighter, or do winds blow colder. The extreme climate of the Antarctic and its remote location on the globe make it an ideal laboratory. Scientific research of such rare conditions may offer the potential to better understand the entire global ecosystem. Because of the efforts of scientists and documentarians, who bring back rare data and footage informing the public about Antarctica's features and ecosystem, the interest among tourists to see and experience this unspoiled place has grown exponentially. Many laud the once-in-a-lifetime trip to Antarctica as experiential education in eco-tourism, a category of traveling focused on environmental conservation and minimal invasiveness on a natural area. Tourism dollars are also a valuable potential source of funds to help finance the many ongoing scientific experiments being conducted. However, despite these benefits, the presence of humans in Antarctica, particularly that of tourists, has been unavoidably intrusive. The sheer number of visitors has resulted in unprecedented damage to the continent, with scientists warning that, unless significant measures are taken, the increasing number of tourists will inevitably bring irreparable future disruptions to the fragile ecosystem there, with possible ripple effects around the world. As Antarctica has no government or rule of law to protect itself, the onus is on scientists, governments, and tour operators to coordinate their efforts to ensure visitors maximize their travel experience without negatively impacting Antarctica's environment.

One of the main problems tourists cause in Antarctica is the disruption of scientific research being conducted there. While scientific study in Antarctica was once the main purpose for human presence there, science seems to have given way to tourism. In fact, from 1990, the number of tourists began to increase to a point where their numbers now exceed the number of scientists (Shaik, 2010). Initially, this was welcomed by research staff whose projects saw a potential funding boost through an increase in visitors, and scientists who stay in Antarctica all year round welcomed the idea of more human contact (Larson, 2012). However, it quickly became apparent that the large number of tourists was beginning to have negative impacts on the scientists. According to American University, which funds research in the Antarctic, independent tour companies are often unaware of research schedules and bring hundreds of tourists to scientific sites requesting explanations and tours (Grall, 1992). In addition, scientific staff sometimes have to stop their work to aid tourists who have either ignored the risks or underestimated the extreme conditions of Antarctica. They have had to participate in the rescue of pilots who crashed attempting to break records, or other adventurers who were not prepared for the harsh exposure while trekking in the cold (Tourists in Antarctica, 2009). All of these disruptions take scientists away from their experiments, cost money, delay important results, and potentially endanger their lives.

A solution to the problem of having scientists attend to the throngs of tourists is increased cooperation between the tour organizers and researchers. Science-based charities or NGOs can actively promote their research facilities as tourist destinations to ensure minimal interference with research projects. In the Canadian low arctic, for example, a research charity attracts, houses, educates, and leads tourists around the area – all under the supervision of experts at the research station. The funds generated in doing this finance the charity and its research while completely controlling the impact of tourists (Churchill Northern, 2007). Likewise, the Chilean government minimizes the impact of tourists who come through their program by confining their visit to its own facilities. Each facility houses and manages the visitors, and the scientists at each station educate and lead tours based on the research focus of each station (Antarctica annual, 2005). By exercising stricter controls and reducing experimental disruptions, operations such as these seem ideal for properly maintaining a workable balance between research and tourism in Antarctica.

Unfortunately, safeguarding scientific efforts in Antarctica amounts to very little if tourists can still disrupt the ecosystem from which all their data are gathered. Therefore, tourism's impact on the ecosystem is perhaps even more worrying than its disruptions of ongoing experiments. The effect that the now nearly 45,000 annual tourists have had on the wildlife in this fragile environment has become a serious concern (Shaik, 2010). Hoping to view the unique animals of the Antarctic, eco-tourists often venture too closely to their habitats or nesting grounds. In addition, although a portion claim to have had some environmental sensitivity training prior to departure, the presence of tourists, regardless of whether they venture too close to the animals or stand at a distance, has been proven to cause stress among the wildlife. Gene S. Fowler (1999), from the University of Washington, documented elevated levels of adrenalin that Magellanic penguins produced upon being excited or scared by a human. It took some birds, especially those that saw humans at irregular intervals, months to recover from their symptoms of shock at these encounters. Similar problems were also found among animals living in areas frequented by humans, even though these animals are presumed by many to be "used to" tourists. According to Trathan, Forcada, Atkinson, Downie, and Shears (2008), the presence of too many humans was the likeliest contributor to a significant drop in gentoo penguin breeding in colonies most exposed to tourists. The delicate balance of natural cues for animals to nest and mate successfully can be all too easily disturbed by the presence of tourists. And the resultant population swings, particularly in an environment as fragile as Antarctica, could directly affect the stability of other animal populations connected through the food chain, leading to a vicious cycle that could reverberate throughout the ecosystem.

Most tour operators do have guidelines for tourists intended to prevent disruption to the ecosystem, but it is apparent that much more needs to be done to ensure guidelines are followed. Over the years, researchers have catalogued increasingly numerous incidents of tourists showing either no knowledge of or complete disregard for the visitor guidelines. Tourists often walked dangerously among Weddell seals on the beach, or ventured to within one foot of a penguin's nest for a photo (Grall, 1992; Shaik, 2010), despite the official guidelines of the International Association of Antarctica Tour Operators (IAATO), which advise no closer than 15 feet (Guidelines, 2012). Similarly, reports of other violations include tourists trying to feed penguins, and numerous incidents of tourists chasing seabirds to make them scatter and fly away for a photo (Trathan et al., 2008). Clearly, the self-regulation of these tour operators is ultimately inadequate in controlling the misdemeanors of tourists. Therefore, regulation should come from the individual governments of the tour operators. Licensing of tour operators should depend on how well they enforce the guidelines for behavior among participants in their tours.

The Antarctic ecosystem is also threatened by environmental hazards brought by the increasing stream of tourists. A number of the tourist cruise ships visiting the area have been damaged by jagged ice, causing oil to gush out into the water. The Associated Press (2007) reported one notable example of a cruise ship which sank in Antarctic waters, releasing over 210,000 liters of diesel, 24,000 liters of lubricant, and 1,000 liters of gasoline into the surrounding water, threatening thousands of penguins en route to the continent for mating season. There has been at least one other report of a ship sinking, and several reports of ships coming too close to shore and running aground (Shaik, 2010). With the presence of more and more vessels, it would only require a few more incidents like these to poison marine life such as krill and plankton, thereby irreparably damaging the food chain. In addition to that from ships, waste from the numerous research and tourist stations pollutes the land. Marcus Zylkstra, an environmentalist in Antarctica, has criticized the condition of a number of American stations as having "decades' worth of human excrement, sewage, gas and oil leaking from broken-down and abandoned vehicles, and numerous piles of discarded garbage and debris" (as cited in Arroyo & Duque, 2004, p. 52). The extent to which biological and chemical pollutants have continued to find their way into the environment shows the lack of responsibility and coordination by the humans using this fragile land.

Moreover, the threat of invasive microbes and other unseen organisms presents a major problem to the safety of the environment. Larson (2012) reports that microbes from foreign environments cling to the boots and jackets of disembarking visitors and infect the flora and fauna in potentially unpredictable ways. Studies have confirmed that virtually every visitor coming to the region carries a plethora of microscopic life forms alien to Antarctica. In addition, tourists unknowingly transport tiny seeds which are carried in their clothing (Askin, 2012). Indeed, Arroyo and Duque (2004) found one invasive species of grass taking root in Antarctica believed to have been introduced via seeds from tourists, and have warned that seeds from "the Iceland Poppy, Tall Fescue Velvet grass and Annual Winter Grass – all from cold climates and capable of growing in Antarctica" (p. 57) have been found, and their spread may threaten the few native grass species. Snyder (2007) further asserted that native Antarctic grass species are particularly vulnerable because they have never had to compete against other species, so they would be easily overrun by the more aggressive invasive strains. Therefore, introducing even just a few organisms of a foreign species is enough to wreak havoc on the ecosystem. In total, the potential for a takeover by invasive species combined with the multitude of environmental pollutants unleashed into the Antarctic environment make human activity a real threat to the entire ecological balance of the continent.

Coordinated efforts between tour operators, their governments, and the scientists stationed in Antarctica could be quite helpful in addressing the threat of environmental hazards. An alliance between scientists and the tourism industry would aid in facilitating the removal of waste produced by humans. The arrival and departure dates could be shared among scientists and tour operators, and tour boats could be responsible for carrying waste with them after they depart. Clearly, the regular removal of biological and other waste would reduce the risk of environmental contamination. Formal cooperation between science and tourism could also decrease the chances of the accidental release of foreign microbes. Tour operators could provide their own outerwear for exclusive use in Antarctica to limit the risk of contamination, and scientists could take further measures to check and disinfect other possessions the tourists might bring. Individual governments can further aid efforts to stop contamination by making strict licensing requirements for the tour operators. Many governments already adhere to the established guidelines for scientific cooperation (Australian Antarctic Division, 2011a; Australian Antarctic Division, 2011b; The Secretariat of the Antarctic Treaty, 2011), and this could act as a basis for all governments involved in Antarctic tourism to cooperatively monitor their tour companies. One especially important requirement is a limit on the number of people allowed to embark on a tour at any one time. Restricting this number would ensure that large ships, which require heavily toxic fuels, are not used in the tours (International Maritime Organization, 2011). Only smaller ships running on lighter and less toxic fuel would be allowed in Antarctic waters, thereby controlling the risk of devastating and irreparable damage to the ecosystem caused by an accident.

In the end, although science was the original reason for the constant presence of humans in Antarctica, the allure of exploring what many consider Earth's last natural frontier is attracting adventurous tourists in increasing numbers. While the arrival of tourists in any part of the world inevitably has its pros and cons, the potential negative effects of tourism on Antarctica, from the disruptions of its wildlife to pollution of its soil and water, could be devastating to the delicate ecosystem. Despite these concerns, tourism need not be stopped. Through cooperation and the strict enforcement of rules, these issues can be overcome so both scientists and tourists may satisfy their interest in Antarctica while minimizing their effect on it. It is only with a concerted effort from all parties involved that Antarctica's pristine environment can be preserved, rather than become a casualty of human self-interest.

References

Antarctica annual turnover 900 million U.S. dollars. (2005, March 31). *MercoPress*. Retrieved from http://en.mercopress.com/2005/03/31/antarctica-annual-turnover-900-million-us-dollars

Arroyo, C. & Duque, H. (2004). Environmental tragedies in the southern reaches: The human impact on Antarctica. *Nuestra Única Tierra*. *3*(1), 46-58.

Askin, P. (2012, March 6). Alien invasion a threat to Antarctic ecosystem. *Reuters*. Retrieved from http://www.reuters.com/article/2012/03/06/us-antarctic-seeds-idUSTRE82504V20120306

Associated Press. (2007, November 6). Sunken Antarctic cruise ship left oil spill. *msnbc.com*. Retrieved from http://www.msnbc.msn.com/id/22039975/

Australian Antarctic Division. (2011a). Australia continues to lead the way in Antarctica. Retrieved from http://www.antarctica.gov.au/media/news/2011/australia-continues-to-lead-the-way-in-antarctica

Australian Antarctic Division. (2011b). Training. Retrieved from http://www.antarctica.gov.au/living-and-working/training

Churchill Northern Studies Centre. (2007, March 7). Unique learning vacations. Retrieved from http://www.churchillscience.ca/index.php?page=vacations

Fowler, G. S. (1999). Behavioral and hormonal responses of Magellanic penguins (Spheniscus magellanicus) to tourism and nest site visitation. *Biological Conservation*, *90*(2), 143–149.

Grall, J. (1992, September). Antarctic tourism impacts. *TED Case Studies*, *2*(1). Retrieved from http://www1.american.edu/TED/antarct.htm

Guidelines for Visitors to the Antarctic (2012). International Association of Antarctica Tour Operators (IAATO). Retrieved from http://iaato.org/c/document_library/get_file?uuid=aed1054d-3e63-4a17-a6cd-a87beb15e287&groupId=10157

International Maritime Organization. (2011, July 29). *Antarctic fuel oil ban and North American ECA MARPOL amendments enter into force on 1 August 2011* [Press Release]. Retrieved from http://www.imo.org/MediaCentre/PressBriefings/Pages/44-MARPOL-amends.aspx

Larson, S. (2012, May 11). More tourists head to Antarctica, affecting the region's ecosystem and science. *Peninsula Press*. Retrieved from http://peninsulapress.com/2012/05/11/more-tourists-head-to-antarctica-affecting-the-regions-ecosystem-and-science/

The Secretariat of the Antarctic Treaty. (2011). Environmental protection. Retrieved from http://www.ats.aq/e/ats_environ.htm

Shaik, A. (2010, May 4). Antarctic wanderlust. *EJ Magazine*, 2010, Spring. Retrieved from http://news.jrn.msu.edu/ejmagazine/2010/05/04/antarctic-wanderlust-a-booming-tourism-industry-may-harm-earth%E2%80%99s-southernmost-continent/

Snyder, J. (2007). Tourism in the polar regions: The sustainability challenge. The United Nations Environment Programme.

Tourists in Antarctica cause of major concern. (2009, December 21). *ScienceDaily*. Retrieved from http://www.sciencedaily.com/releases/2009/12/091221130220.htm

Trathan, P. N., Forcada, J., Atkinson, R., Downie, R. H., & Shears, J. R. (2008). Population assessments of gentoo penguins (Pygoscelis papua) breeding at an important Antarctic tourist site, Goudier Island, Port Lockroy, Palmer Archipelago, Antarctica. *Biological Conservation, 141*(12), 3019–3028.

Part 3 Logical fallacies

Part 2 introduced how to develop controlling ideas using claims, evidence, and explanations. It is essential that these arguments are developed logically. Mistakes with the logical connections in an argument are known as logical fallacies and should be avoided when writing an essay.

In general, logical fallacies result from:

1. **overgeneralization** – the reason and/or the conclusion are too broad to be accurate.
2. **irrelevance** – the reason for the conclusion is not relevant.

Section 1 Overgeneralization

1. Fallacy of division

The characteristics of a small sample are inaccurately transferred to a whole group.

Examples:

Because the minister of finance was discovered to be corrupt, the public should not trust politicians.

This argument assumes that because one politician is corrupt, all politicians are therefore corrupt.

Since the majority of drug traffickers are foreigners, the government should impose restrictions on the number of immigrants allowed into the country.

Not every foreigner is a drug trafficker, but the illegal actions of a few are leading to demands for sweeping regulations for all foreigners.

2. False cause

The cause of something has not been proven or cannot be proven.

Examples:

People are unemployed because they do not want to accept jobs which pay low wages.

There may be many causes of unemployment, such as lack of job experience, poor education, or few job opportunities. Essay topics often deal with complex problems which cannot be explained with one definitive reason.

The number of people visiting a psychologist regularly has increased significantly since the introduction of Freud's theories at the beginning of the twentieth century. This shows that psychotherapy is an effective treatment for mental illnesses.

This argument claims that a rise in people seeing psychologists means that psychotherapy is effective. However, this conclusion is an overgeneralization about the cause of this rise. The effectiveness of psychotherapy often depends more on the results of the therapy rather than the number of people visiting therapists. Moreover, a rise in the number of people in therapy could be attributable to a population increase, or perhaps an increase in stress in people's lives.

3. False dichotomy

Only two options are presented, "either X or Y." However, in reality more than two options exist.

Examples:

In order to prevent an increase in the number of road users, it is essential to reduce public transportation fees. The alternative to a fee reduction is congestion and delays resulting from an increase in traffic.

This argument presents reducing fees as one option, and the only other option (or result) will be increased congestion. However, other measures to reduce congestion are possible.

Those who are proficient English speakers are likely to be prepared for the intense negotiations involved in global business, while those who are not proficient at English are bound to succumb to the pressures of international negotiations.

This argument assumes that there are only two types of people – a good negotiator who is proficient at English and a poor negotiator who is not proficient at English. However, such an overgeneralization ignores the other skills necessary to be a good negotiator, such as the ability to think logically, to empathize with one's counterpart, and to make proposals which may bring agreement.

Exercise 1 **Identify the logical fallacy in the following examples.**

1. Another significant teenage health issue the government should address is alcohol consumption. Health care professionals report increasing alcohol consumption among teenagers. This is particularly a problem because in some cases it leads to violence, absenteeism from school, and criminal behavior such as vandalism (Report on youth, 2004). It is important that the government increase awareness among young people of the dangers that may come from excessive drinking. Without this kind of preventative education, the problem will increase. Special government-appointed health advisors in schools should provide detailed lectures to all high school students which promote a better understanding of the effects of alcohol on the human body. This should be supplemented by an advertising campaign in which popular celebrities clearly explain the reasons for the legal drinking age and highlight the negative effects of alcohol on teenage bodies.

2. The increase in levels of violence portrayed in movies is well documented. Furthermore, research by Wills and Stanford (2008) shows that in the highest grossing movies of the 1990s, the immediate consequences of violence were portrayed significantly less than in previous decades. They conclude that "the role of violence in blockbuster movies moved from a plot device to merely an additional element of entertainment." This produced a kind of cultural desensitization to violence which led to an increase in the number of violent assaults in urban areas during the same time period.

3. One source of environmental damage is industrial pollution to rivers. A 2008 investigation by the Organization for Nature Protection described the case of a large textile company polluting the environment. This company was found to have released amounts of chemicals into nearby rivers which were above the limits set by law. Examples such as this demonstrate that more significant punishments need to be put in place to make sure that large companies follow legal guidelines.

Section 2 Irrelevance

1. Straw man

The opposing argument is represented inaccurately so it can be easily defeated.

Examples:

The reason that people support the decision to wage war is because they wish to see the destruction of other countries.

This is an extreme representation of the opinions of people who support wars. It is likely to be untrue.

Public works projects such as bridges, highways, tunnels, and dams are an ideal way to keep a country's population employed. People opposed to such types of government spending probably put nature over the welfare of the population.

It is inaccurate to claim that those opposed to government spending on public works projects don't care about people's welfare. They may simply believe that this kind of spending is wasteful, and that there are better ways the money could be used to keep people employed.

2. Slippery slope

The argument assumes that one thing occurring will inevitably lead to a number of other things occurring.

Examples:

Taxpayers will suffer if the government increases wages for teachers because it will eventually increase wages for every other kind of public servant. This will cost a huge amount of money taxpayers cannot afford.

If the government raises teachers' wages, it does not automatically mean that it will have to raise the wages of other kinds of public servants. The argument would be improved if the conclusion was less extreme. It would also be improved if it explained how raising wages of one group of public servants could lead to pressure to raise the wages of other public servants who feel they also deserve raises.

If same sex marriage is permitted, then soon traditional families will cease to exist.

This argument assumes that if same sex couples are allowed to marry, it will cause a chain of events that will make traditional marriages disappear. This is illogical.

3. False appeal

An unrelated authority or reason is cited to support an argument.

Examples:

Children should learn to play soccer at school because it is the most popular sport in the world.

Just because an activity is popular is not a sufficient reason to do it. Further evidence should be provided (e.g., the possible health or social benefits of playing soccer).

One way to improve education in high school is to replace traditional textbooks with tablet computers. In fact, a survey showed that 95 percent of high school students support such an idea.

While high school students may have some valid ideas on how to improve education, they may have a variety of reasons for wanting a tablet computer not necessarily education related (e.g., to play games, to not have to carry a load of books). There are other people who are likely to have more knowledge on whether or not using tablet computers in classrooms would actually improve education, such as educational researchers and teachers.

4. Circular reasoning

The conclusion is the same as the original argument.

Examples:
She was elected because she was the most popular choice among voters.

Being elected is the same as being most popular among voters. The argument needs to explain why she is popular with voters.

Becoming bilingual should be a requirement for all foreign ministers, as they will be able to speak two languages.

Speaking two languages is the definition of bilingualism. An explanation of why bilingualism should be required by foreign ministries needs to be provided.

5. Non-sequitur

There is no connection or a very weak connection between the reason and the conclusion.

Examples:
The previous financial recession was caused by rapid inflation. Therefore, the current recession cannot be the result of low wages.

The fact that a past recession was caused by one factor does not mean that a current recession cannot be caused by a different reason.

Japan's population began declining as the country became more affluent and more women became educated and career-minded. It stands to reason, then, that with more wealth and improved educational and employment opportunities for women, countries in Africa will experience a population decline.

Population trends are caused by a complex variety of factors specific to a country. It is not logical to assume that the circumstances in Japan will be the same all over Africa.

Exercise 2

Identify the logical fallacy in the following paragraphs and suggest a way to improve the argument.

1. Figures from elementary school exams demonstrate that grades in mathematics have been at a record low for the last three years. Consequently, the Ministry of Education needs to make mathematics the primary focus of elementary school education. Mathematics is necessary for many important everyday tasks, such as purchasing goods, deciding journey times, and checking salary payments. If young children are not taught the foundations of mathematics, they will carry this weakness over as they grow older, and after they graduate from school and enter society, they will carry out daily tasks inefficiently, resulting in many wasted hours of work time.

2. Major media companies are applying pressure on official legislative bodies to impose stricter fines – and even prison sentences – on individuals who download copyrighted material. Despite the argument from media companies that current laws are not effective, increasing punishments would be too extreme. There is a widespread consensus that the existing legal boundaries are fair. Public opinion surveys from the past decade demonstrate that between 60 and 70 percent of the population support the existing copyright laws.

3. The evidence suggests that the most effective way to help a country win more medals at the Olympic Games is to recruit children who show great promise as athletes. These children could be placed in special training academies, which would accelerate the improvement of their skills to a world-class level quickly and effectively. However, some people disagree with this proposal because they lack a sense of patriotism, as shown by their lack of concern for their country's success in international sports competitions.

4. Basketball has shown itself to be an enduringly popular spectator sport. The appeal of watching basketball lies in the game's high scores. *Sports Eye* magazine reports that an average of 83 points has been scored per game over the previous five seasons (8). Fans enjoy watching teams score continuously throughout the game. It is precisely these high scores that attract fans of all ages to the sport.

5. One area in which zoos are particularly useful is for schoolchildren. For instance, it is common for classes of children to visit zoos to get practical experience which supplements what they are learning about in biology classes. Indeed, many zoos offer discounts for groups of students in order to encourage their use as an educational tool. Prices may be lowered by up to 50 percent if groups of students are accompanied by a teacher. As a result, children can receive information and education that they would not be able to find in textbooks.

Exercise 3

Identify the reasons and conclusions in the following arguments. Decide whether or not they contain logical fallacies.

Example:

In a recent survey of university students, almost half reported spending more time doing club activities than preparing for classes. Clearly, university students do not feel that the information they are learning in their classes is valuable.

Reason: Half of students spend more time on club activities than preparation.

Conclusion: Students do not feel classes are valuable.

This is a false cause. The evidence does not provide reasons why students spend more time on club activities. Some students may feel that the contents of their classes are not valuable, but there are many other reasons affecting how students choose to use their time.

1. The right of police officers to carry weapons became a controversial issue last week after the police shot and killed an unarmed man. It can be argued that police officers require more training before they can be allowed to do police work. Their current training has been shown to be inadequate.

   Reason: ______________________

   Conclusion: ______________________

   ____

   ____

   ____

2. U.S. military spending accounts for approximately 40 percent of total military expenditure in the world, more than four times the amount of the next biggest country. This is why the United States is the strongest military power in the world.

   Reason: ______________________

   Conclusion: ______________________

   ____

   ____

   ____

3. Cycling is a less environmentally damaging method of transportation compared to driving. Employees who cycle to work are more concerned about environmental matters than people who live a similar distance from work but drive to their offices.

Reason: ______________________________

Conclusion: ______________________________

____

____

____

4. Many companies have a policy of encouraging traditional styles of gray and black clothing during the autumn season. However, fashion designer Clare Hall believes that the pastel autumn colors are also suitable for casual business environments. It is time for companies to change the limited view of what constitutes appropriate business attire.

Reason: ______________________________

Conclusion: ______________________________

____

____

____

5. Many teachers in public schools are unhappy with their working conditions, so if the government does not increase wages for teachers, many of them will quit and search for jobs in other fields.

Reason: ______________________________

Conclusion: ______________________________

____

____

____

6. A rise in student exam scores over the last few years demonstrates that these examinations have become easier.

Reason: ______________________________

Conclusion: ______________________________

____

____

____

7. Windows is a superior computer operating system because it is the biggest selling and most widely used computer system in the world.

Reason: ______________________

Conclusion: ______________________

____

____

____

8. Four of the top 20 countries in Asia in terms of gross domestic product (GDP) are Japan, China, Korea, and Malaysia. This shows how vital exports are to this region of the world.

Reason: ______________________

Conclusion: ______________________

____

____

____

9. As the possibility of illegal music downloading has increased, revenues from CD sales have dropped steadily. Therefore, music companies could increase CD sales by convincing governments to introduce measures to reduce levels of illegal downloading.

Reason: ______________________

Conclusion: ______________________

____

____

____

10. The U.N. has reported that industrialized countries waste 30 percent of edible food annually while over one billion people living in poverty are unable to get enough to eat every day. Reducing food waste will help alleviate the problem of the starving poor.

Reason: ______________________

Conclusion: ______________________

____

____

____

Part

4 Concluding paragraphs

The concluding paragraph signals to readers that the essay is coming to a close. An effective conclusion reinforces the essay's arguments and leaves a positive final impression on the reader. In fact, the conclusion is often what readers remember the most, as it is the last thing they read.

The concluding paragraph:

1. reminds the reader of the position in the thesis and the main points from each paragraph.
2. leaves the reader with a final thought.

Below is the concluding paragraph from the essay on page 53.

Position / main points

In the end, although science was the original reason for the constant presence of humans in Antarctica, the allure of exploring what many consider Earth's last natural frontier is attracting adventurous tourists in increasing numbers. While the arrival of tourists in any part of the world inevitably has its pros and cons, the potential negative effects of tourism on Antarctica, from the disruptions of its wildlife to pollution of its soil and water, could be devastating to the delicate ecosystem. Despite these concerns, tourism need not be stopped. Through cooperation and the strict enforcement of rules, these issues can be overcome so both scientists and tourists may satisfy their interest in Antarctica while minimizing their effect on it. It is only with a concerted effort from all parties involved that

Final thought → Antarctica's pristine environment can be preserved, rather than become a casualty of human self-interest.

Section 1 An effective final thought

The following techniques and examples show how effective conclusions can be made.

1. Re-emphasize the importance of the issue or the position taken:
   It is only with a concerted effort from all parties involved that Antarctica's pristine environment can be preserved, rather than become a casualty of human self-interest.

2. Make a prediction based on the facts:
   However, if no effort is made to mitigate the harmful effects tourism is causing on Antarctica, future scientists may be left researching environmental destruction rather than environmental purity.

3. Make a recommendation for further action:
   Ultimately, individual governments of countries from which tours originate will need to take the lead and enforce harsher penalties to ensure protection is not compromised for the sake of profit.

4. Assess the value of the arguments in the essay:
   Human presence is bound to alter Antarctica's landscape and ecosystem to some degree, but exclusion is neither practical nor desirable. Therefore, given the circumstances, coordinated efforts will surely help guarantee Antarctica's purity can be explored and enjoyed by future generations of scientists and tourists.

Section 2 What to avoid in the concluding paragraph

The following information is not suitable in a concluding paragraph:

1. New information – the conclusion should focus on only the arguments presented in the body of the essay. Any new information will distract the reader and reduce the impact of the essay.

   For example:
   Global warming is sure to increase if nothing is done to protect Antarctica.
   (No mention was made in the essay of global warming, so mentioning it in the conclusion is inappropriate.)

2. Empty statements – avoid obvious statements that the reader already knows and vague statements which do not say anything about the topic.

   For example:
   The evidence shows that tourism in Antarctica is a difficult problem.
   (Most issues worthy of academic analysis are difficult to solve, so there is no need to state the obvious.)

   Nature is a precious resource that is important for everyone.
   (This point is obvious and offers no further insight.)

Exercise 1

These concluding paragraphs relate to the introductory paragraphs in Exercise 4 on page 38. Write an effective final thought for each.

1. As the evidence shows, more companies which had traditionally been seniority-based are switching to a merit-based system to determine pay and position. While such moves are sure to initially create resentment and fear among employees accustomed to a seniority-based system, guaranteeing lifetime employment seems to no longer be suitable in a global economy, where even formerly domestically focused companies must bow to the pressure to be efficient and flexible in order to simply stay in business.

2. In conclusion, Keynesian economic policy still seems to hold merit in mitigating the severity of an economic recession. As has been demonstrated, recessions are tending to last longer than before, due to company and consumer behavior which is driven by the fear that the media perpetuates. Therefore, it is apparent that future economic downturns will likely require more radical and severe government interventions to combat this fear before a turnaround can be realized.

3. Indeed, the far-reaching impact of hip-hop culture is due to a number of factors which demonstrate its relevance to young people all around the globe. While the marketing power of the hip-hop industry is evident in the amount of money it generates, its appeal in regions as diverse as the U.K., Myanmar, and the Middle East indicates that resistance to authority and desire for change are themes common to youth everywhere.

UNIT 3

Using and Citing Sources

Part

1 Evaluating sources

Section 1 Primary, secondary, and tertiary sources

Information from sources is necessary in academic writing to support the writer's ideas and arguments. Sources can be grouped into three basic types: primary, secondary, and tertiary. Each type can provide important information to the essay writer when researching and writing essays.

A **primary source** is where information (e.g., statistics, research results) originally comes from. Some of the more common primary sources cited in academic essays are:

- **A scholarly / professional journal** – Journal articles are usually written by experts in a field and are reviewed by other experts before being published.
- **A government organization** – Government organizations usually have the resources and expertise to provide official information (e.g., data on the population, crime, the economy)
- **A reputable organization** – Well-known and respected organizations (e.g., UNESCO, WHO, OECD, the World Bank) often have resources and expertise that allow them to provide reliable information.
- **A university** – Universities publish information by knowledgeable professionals with expertise in their fields.
- **An expert** – Experts in fields make comments through speeches, interviews, editorials, or books.

In an academic essay, try to use the primary source of information, especially for facts, statistics, and research results.

A **secondary source** reports or interprets information from primary sources, such as articles in magazines and newspapers, or postings on a website. For example, look at the following excerpt from an article published in a newspaper:

> *Many people are worried that the aging population is causing roads to become more dangerous. Statistics from the Department of Transportation show that of the over 5,000 traffic accidents last year which resulted in at least one death, nearly a quarter were caused by drivers 65 or older, the highest of any age group categorized. This has prompted the state government to consider adopting stricter regulations for the licensing of elderly drivers.*

The newspaper is a secondary source that is reporting statistics on traffic accidents, but the primary source of these statistics is the "Department of Transportation."

Secondary sources can be useful in academic writing, especially when another person's interpretation of information from a primary source is required.

NOTE: A newspaper or magazine can be considered a primary source in some instances (e.g., an interview with a witness to an event, a commentary from an expert on a particular topic, or a past issue of a newspaper or magazine for historical research.)

A **tertiary source** is a collection of information from primary and secondary sources which often offers a condensed description of a topic. Examples of tertiary sources are encyclopedias, guidebooks, indices, and textbooks.

Tertiary sources are not usually accepted as appropriate sources in academic writing because much of their information comes from primary or secondary sources. However, they can be useful because they provide background information on topics, and they do provide a reference list of primary and secondary sources on the topic to help essay writers begin their research.

Exercise 1

Read the model essay on tourism in Antarctica on page 53. Find the sources used in the essay, and decide which are primary and which are secondary.

Determining credibility

All sources need to be evaluated to determine how useful their information can be in an essay. The following aspects of each source need to be evaluated.

1. Author (person or organization)

- Who is the author of the information?
- What expertise or reputation does this author have?

2. Publisher

- Who published the information?

NOTES:
1. Even if the author of the information is unknown, a respected publisher probably means the information is credible.
2. For internet sources, the publisher is normally the server where the information is stored, so this does not ensure that the information is reliable.

3. Purpose

- Who was the information written for?
- Is the author making an argument, making a criticism, or just stating facts on a topic?
- What is the author's motivation – why was the information written?

4. Accuracy

- Is there credible evidence to support the ideas presented in the information?
- Does the information lean only towards one viewpoint or does it consider multiple viewpoints?
- Are there other sources used in the information, and are they identified in-text or in a list of references?
- For internet sources, are there hyperlinks to other sources?

5. Context

- When was the source originally published?
- Has it been revised or updated – is the information still relevant to the topic?
- Were any significant events happening in society when the source was written? Could those events have influenced the source in some way?
- Does the source seem unique in its position on the topic compared to other sources?
- Is the writing style and tone similar to or different from other sources?

Part

2 Integrating source information

Section 1 Paraphrasing, summarizing, and quoting

There are three methods to integrate source information: **paraphrases**, **summaries**, and **quotations**.

- **Paraphrases** – specific details of source information are written in the writer's own words and style.
- **Summaries** – the main idea of source information is written in the writer's own words and style in significantly fewer words than the original source.
- **Quotations** – source information is written using the exact words as the original source and placed inside quotation marks.

NOTE: Paraphrases, summaries, and quotations are the first steps in avoiding **plagiarism**: copying of other people's words and ideas and using them as your own. This is viewed as stealing and could have serious consequences. By rewriting source information in paraphrases and summaries, essay writers avoid copying others' words; in using quotations, essay writers indicate that words were copied, and that they belong to someone else. Combining these three techniques with citation (see Part 3) is necessary anytime outside sources are used in an essay.

Choosing to paraphrase or summarize

Paraphrase or summarize when the source information is useful, but its exact wording is not important. The choice to paraphrase or summarize also depends on the amount of detail required from the source:

- If useful source information is up to about 50 words, then paraphrase. Paraphrasing longer passages is ineffective because it moves the focus of the essay from the writer's ideas to other people's ideas.
- If useful source information is over 50 words, and only the main ideas are useful, then summarize.

Shared language

Before writing a paraphrase or summary, identify shared language in the source. Shared language is words and phrases that cannot be effectively expressed in another way. When paraphrasing and summarizing, shared language does not need to be reworded because it is not unique to the original writer or source, and is necessary to maintain meaning.

Many words and phrases can be shared language. A few examples are:

- Proper nouns
  the Olympics, the United Nations, Mount Kinabalu, Alexander the Great
- Common nouns
  lion, banana, election, culture, hydrogen
- Dates and figures
  1972, 25%, 37 million
- Specialized language / terminologies
  public opinion, gross national product, chemical reaction

NOTE: Some shared language can have their word forms changed but maintain the meaning of the original. The word "election" could be changed to "elected," depending on how the writer rewrites the information. For example:

She won the election because of her business career.
Her background in business is why she was elected.

Exercise 1

Underline the shared language in the following passage.

Spanish conquistadors discovered potatoes in Peru in the sixteenth century. They were soon introduced to Europe where they became the staple food in many regions. Some historians believe that the potato, a highly reliable and nutritious crop, eliminated a major source of civil unrest: famine. This led to healthier and increased populations, which in turn resulted in much more stable governments and economies. With this stability, a number of European countries were able to increase their power and eventually project it around the world between 1700 and 1950. In short, the potato was instrumental in helping create the great European empires.

Section 2 Writing paraphrases and summaries

1. Six steps to writing a paraphrase

1. Read the passage several times until you understand its meaning fully.
2. On a separate piece of paper, note down the ideas from the passage in the order they appeared in the original and underline the shared language.
3. Avoiding the first idea from the source, choose one of the other ideas to start the paraphrase.
4. Without looking at the original text, use your notes to write the paraphrase.

5. Keep the shared language, but change the wording of the original using different:
   - words (a thesaurus will help).
   - word forms (a dictionary will help).
   - grammatical structure.
   - word order.

   However, do not:
   - change the verb tense of the original.
   - change meaning or add ideas not in the original.
   - use more than three words in a row from the original text without quotation marks. (Using more than three words in a row without quoting is considered plagiarism.)
6. Check the paraphrase against the original passage to ensure:
   - the same meaning is conveyed.
   - the paraphrase is not plagiarized.

   Revise the paraphrase if necessary.

Example:

1. Read the original:

   "Increases in the cost of air travel have had a negative effect on tourism in destinations such as Hawaii, which are significant distances from other countries."

2. Note down ideas in the order they appeared in the original and underline shared language:

   Increases cost air travel / negative effect / tourism in destinations Hawaii / significant distances from other countries.

3. Choose a different idea from the first to begin the paraphrase:

   Increases cost air travel / negative effect / tourism in destinations Hawaii / significant distances from other countries.

4. Write the paraphrase using your notes:

   The tourist industry in places like Hawaii, which is fairly remote from other countries, has been adversely affected by rises in airfare.

5. Keep the shared language, but change the wording of the original. Note in the paraphrase: "destinations" changed to "places," "significant distances" changed to "fairly remote," and "have a negative effect" changed to "adversely affected." The tense of the paraphrase is the same as the original.

6. Check the paraphrase against the original passage to ensure the same meaning is conveyed and the paraphrase is not plagiarized.

2. Five steps to writing a summary

1. Read the information to be summarized several times until you understand its meaning fully.

2. On a separate piece of paper, note down the main points of the original source and underline the shared language. To help identify the main points:
   - In longer texts, pay attention to the introductory and concluding paragraphs, chapter or paragraph headings, and topic and concluding sentences in paragraphs – they often help in identifying main ideas.
   - In longer sources of information, write a few key words for each paragraph summarizing the content.
   - In the original text:
     - Words and phrases like *in summary*, *in short*, *basically*, and *in other words* can be useful.
     - Information following phrases like *for example ...*, *such as ...*, *for instance ...* is normally not a main point, so it should not be used in a summary.
     - Quotes in the original source are also used to support the writer's main point, so they should not be used in the summary.
3. Without looking at the original, write the summary using only your notes. Use any necessary shared language.
4. Check the summary against the original passage to ensure the main idea is conveyed and the summary is not plagiarized (see paraphrase, step 5).
5. Revise the summary if necessary. The summary should be much shorter than the original – often only one or two sentences in length.

Example:

1. Read the original.

> The 1984 Olympics in Los Angeles demonstrated the considerable political value of sporting events during the Cold War. The 1984 Games took place against a backdrop of the key political issues of the time. The 1980 Moscow Olympics had been boycotted by the USA, and many of its client states, in protest over the Soviet invasion of Afghanistan in 1979. The Soviet Union and 16 other countries boycotted the 1984 Olympics, although intense U.S. diplomacy ensured China and Romania sent teams (Hill, 1999). The Games still attracted 6,802 competitors from 140 countries, competing across 221 different events (Toohey & Veal, 2000). This political opportunity was seized upon by the 1984 organizers. The noted French political economist Jean-August Sevigny (2001) wrote, "The tit-for-tat boycotts made the LA Olympics a perfect opportunity to upstage the Soviet enemy and display all that was good – and better – about the USA" (p. 12). For the first time, official large-scale commercial Olympic sponsorship was allowed, major corporate funding was accepted for the building of certain facilities, and exclusive TV broadcast rights were secured by the highest bidders. Rampant commercialism undoubtedly, but the 1984 Olympics registered a healthy $223 million profit (Davis, 2012). And with the organizers promoting the L.A. Olympics as a patriotic display of Americanism, the 1984 Games served as an ideal showcase for the vibrancy of U.S. consumer society in the context of the ongoing Cold War.

2. On a separate piece of paper, write down the main points of the original source and underline any shared language:

   1984 Olympics Los Angeles, political value, Cold War / 1980 Moscow Olympics boycotted by USA / Soviet invasion Afghanistan / Soviets and others boycotted 1984 L.A. / opportunity to upstage Soviet, display good/ better about USA / First time – commercial sponsorship, corporate funding, TV broadcast highest bidder = commercialism / $223 million profit, patriotic display Americanism, vibrancy U.S. consumer

3. Without looking at the original, write the summary using only your notes. Use any necessary shared language:

   Despite the Soviet Union and some of its allies boycotting the 1984 Olympics in Los Angeles in response to the U.S.'s boycott four years earlier of the Moscow Olympics over the Soviet's invasion of Afghanistan in 1979, the L.A. Olympics were politically successful in making the Soviets jealous of the U.S.'s commercial power which was displayed through commercial sponsorships, corporate funding, and TV broadcast rights bidding. As a result, the animosity between the two countries intensified.

4. Check the summary against the original passage to ensure the main idea is conveyed and the summary is not plagiarized.

   Despite the Soviet Union and some of its allies boycotting the 1984 Olympics in Los Angeles ~~in response to the U.S.'s boycott four years earlier of the Moscow Olympics over the Soviet's invasion of Afghanistan in 1979~~, the L.A. Olympics were politically successful in ~~making the Soviets jealous~~ of the U.S.'s commercial power which was displayed through ~~commercial sponsorships, corporate funding, and TV broadcast rights bidding.~~ As a result, ~~the animosity between the two countries intensified.~~

   Cut – not part of main idea

   Inaccurate

   Cut – details too minute + too close to plagiarism (same words and word order)

   Inaccurate

5. Revise the summary if necessary. The summary should be much shorter than the original – often only one or two sentences in length:

   Despite a boycott from the Soviet Union and some allies, the 1984 Los Angeles Olympics were a political success in the midst of the Cold War as the U.S. could show the power of commercialism and the advantages of being American.

Exercise 2

Read the following passage. The underlined parts in the original source information have been plagiarized in the paraphrase and summary. Find and underline the plagiarized parts in the paraphrase and summary.

Original source information

"The modern concept of democracy is the result of an evolution begun by the ancient Greeks. For the Greeks, however, democracy was a right exercised only by the elite – landowning men, a fraction of the population. Non-landowning men, and women were normally excluded from any political involvement and were disenfranchised. Yet this condition was not believed to be a restriction on freedom, but rather a reflection of society's values. Those of wealth and status were expected to hold the reigns of power, as it was their inherited right and responsibility to attend to the affairs of state."

Plagiarized paraphrase

Contemporary society's idea of democracy began in ancient times with the Greeks. However, for the Greeks democracy was a right exercised only by a fraction of the population – landowning men. This elite prohibited men without property and women from voting or having any kind of political involvement. However, this situation was a reflection of society's values and not believed to be a restriction on freedom. To the ancient Greeks, the elite had the responsibility to wield power over all society because they possessed wealth and position, and this gave them an inherited right and responsibility to control the government.

Plagiarized summary

As a reflection of society's values, the ancient Greeks believed that only those of wealth and status were expected to govern.

Exercise 3

Below are an acceptable paraphrase and summary of the original passage from Exercise 3. In each, find and underline the rewording of the plagiarized parts.

Acceptable paraphrase

To the ancient Greeks, democracy meant that those possessing high social rank – a minute percentage of society – had the duty to lead the state. Yet, rather than seeing this arrangement as a limitation of freedom, those excluded from political involvement, such as women and men without property, accepted it as an extension of the natural social order. Therefore, though contemporary democracy has evolved from ancient times, in its very early form, only the elite (normally landowning men) governed the entire state.

Acceptable summary

The ancient Greeks believed that only men occupying society's highest class had the right and duty to govern in a democracy.

Exercise 4

Choose the best paraphrase of the original text.

Original passage

"Although white rice accounts for 35–80% of the caloric intake for 3.3 billion Asians, it has several problems, such as a lack of adequate nutrition, which makes Asians' body size relatively small; and also a lack of taste, which leads to a high consumption of sodium in many of the foods eaten with rice."

Paraphrases

a. The over 3 billion Asians whose calories mostly come from white rice should change their diet because white rice is nutritionally deficient, making them smaller than other races, and also tasteless, causing people to add more sodium to the other foods they eat with rice.

b. Nutritional deficiency and tastelessness are two aspects of white rice which make it a less than ideal food for those whose calories are heavily dependent on it, which includes other 3 billion Asians, who have small bodies and consume a lot of sodium as a result.

c. Although rice supplies 35–80% of the calories eaten by 3.3 billion Asians, it makes Asians weaker because of the lack of nutrition "and high sodium in other foods."

Exercise 5

Paraphrase the following passages on a separate piece of paper.

1. Because it is portable and inexpensive, ultrasound equipment is used in some traditional societies to identify the sex of the fetus, and abort unwanted girls.

2. Over-population, pollution, climate change, poor sanitation, and rising sea levels are contributing to a scarcity of fresh water. Over the long-term, this scarcity could become a crisis for the world, causing wars as billions of people will compete over access to vital fresh water supplies in the future.

3. Alan Turing is widely seen as the "Father of Computing." While studying at Cambridge, Turing introduced the concept of the algorithm, the idea at the heart of modern computing. In 1950, Turing also proposed the idea of artificial intelligence: the ability for machines to think.

4. In 2011, Africa became the largest cellular phone market after Asia. With 600 million users, the size and quality of Africa's cellular network is developing rapidly to meet the growing demand of users.

5. The fact that certain blood types are more vulnerable to particular kinds of diseases is proven, but there has never been any credible research that links blood types to certain personality traits.

Exercise 6

Choose the best summary of the original text.

Original passage

Some educators maintain that choosing a major is the most crucial decision for students entering college, whereas others argue it is not especially important. Paul Harrington, Neeta Fogg, and Thomas Harrington argue in *College Majors Handbook* that as the world becomes more competitive, those students with a clear career path on entering college have an obvious advantage over those who do not. Those who want to pursue high-paying careers such as medicine or engineering ought to focus on their career goal as early as possible. It is a mistake for students to start college with the aim of working out what they want to do for the rest of their lives, the authors argue. However, Donald Asher in his book, *How to Get a Job with Any Major*, disagrees. The choice of major often does not limit a student's career options. Although there are certain majors that clearly prepare students for particular careers, most students ultimately pursue careers unrelated to their chosen major. Asher believes that students can best spend their time in university finding their true interests because, on average, people switch careers, often to something completely unrelated, three to five times in their working lives.

a. Some educationalists contend that deciding on a major is the most critical decision students face when entering college, whereas others argue that the most important thing for students to discover in university is their true interests, because many establish careers not related to the major they studied in college.

b. Students who spend their college time working out what to do in the future are at a disadvantage in an increasingly competitive world compared with those who are motivated to set career goals and choose a major to achieve them.

c. Educators disagree over the importance of choosing a major: some believe it is crucial in giving students an advantage in an increasingly competitive world, while others argue that as people usually end up in careers unrelated to their college major and change careers several times, having a major is not especially important.

Exercise 7

Summarize the following passages on a separate piece of paper.

1. In their theory about the nature and origin of crime, Travis Hirshi and Michael Gottfredson dismiss the older notion of "indirect control," the "psychological presence" parents possessed in the minds of their children, to explain the inherent barriers to deviancy. Instead, the centrality of "self-control" in explaining the propensity to commit or refrain from crime is advanced. The authors maintain that this accounts for all factors – whether age, culture, sex, or circumstances – in determining whether someone commits a crime or not. A child develops self-control through direct parenting, when the parent closely monitors the child's behavior and punishes deviancy when it occurs. Without it, lack of self-control develops naturally. People who develop low self-control in childhood are more likely to act on an urge to break laws, should the opportunity exist. Crucially, an individual's tendency to commit crime is shaped by his/her lack of self-control, not the ease and availability of opportunities to engage in crime. Further, low self-control promotes an outlook on life as a "permanent present" in which immediate gratification is central. To such people, crime supplies immediate risks, thrills, and rewards.

2. The electric guitar became important to other music genres, although in no other genre did it take on the significance it did in rock and roll. The ability of the electric guitar to distort, alter, and sustain notes was picked up by country, blues, and jazz musicians. Yet it was not until rock and roll emerged from the 1950s that the electric guitar gained widespread appeal. Rock and roll devotees marveled at the range of sounds and volumes the electric guitar could produce and saw its huge potential, both musically and within the broader counter-culture of the decades after World War II. The image of the rock and roller with his leather jacket and slicked-back hair was never complete without him holding an electric guitar. Curiously, despite its current place within the mainstream music culture, the electric guitar was initially treated with great skepticism by traditional audiences and instrument makers in the music world. How wrong they were! The electric guitar has come to embody a musical genre, a generation, a set of values, and even a way of life.

3. What is becoming clearer is the disjuncture between advancing technology and our ability to manage its wider repercussions. Social networking services (SNS) like Facebook and LinkedIn increasingly dominate people's time online. Data shows that 66% of the 80% of Americans who use the internet use social networking services; and of the 95% of teenagers in the U.S. on the internet, 80% of them use SNS. Social networks have started to supplement, even replace, face-to-face relationships. For many of Facebook's 901 million monthly worldwide users, the role of SNS in friendship goes beyond simply getting in touch and keeping in touch. Social networking online involves a level of public display and self-promotion entirely new to the majority of people. SNS leaves the nuances of emotion unexplored or unarticulated, and the gradual process of getting to know someone – the true beauty of friendship – are fast-tracked, as everything, quite literally, is on their SNS profile.

Section 3 Using quotations

In general, quoting a source can be useful when the information is:

- from a respected authority on the topic.
- written in a particularly powerful or memorable way.
- from a primary source.
- mostly shared language which cannot be effectively rewritten.

Do not rely on quotations as the main method to include source information in an essay. Overusing quotations makes it seem like the essay is just repeating someone else's words and ideas. In general, essay writers should express ideas using their own words whenever possible. Therefore, quotations are best used strategically to help emphasize information.

How a quotation is introduced is also important. The introduction should:

- indicate the quote's significance.
- prepare the reader for the sudden change in writing style.

Example:

Thesis:

Although colonization in general is seen as cross-cultural bullying, colonization by the West has brought about changes that have shaped the state of society in certain parts of the world.

Body paragraph excerpt:

... colonization by the British Empire often resulted in the mistreatment of the indigenous population. "In India, colonialism of course was seen as dehumanizing. Being suppressed and discriminated against in your own land is beyond humiliating" (Joshi, 45).

In the excerpt above, the sentence before the first quotation mentions *the mistreatment of the indigenous population.* Therefore, the reader may expect evidence following this statement to show how indigenous populations were mistreated. However, the quotation is about feelings associated with mistreatment – *dehumanizing* and *humiliating* – which is a sudden change for the reader.

The quotation should be introduced more effectively to better prepare the reader:

Colonization by the British Empire often resulted in the mistreatment of the indigenous population. Sanjay Joshi, a researcher at the Mumbai Language Institute, emphasized the sentiment felt by many who were colonized: "In India, colonialism of course was seen as dehumanizing. Being suppressed and discriminated against in your own land is beyond humiliating" (45).

The introduction prepared readers for the quote by indicating the content – *the sentiment felt*.

Note also how source details are mentioned in the introducing sentence to show that the source is an Indian person, which gives authority to his description of the feelings of Indian people.

Integrating quotations

Below are some techniques to integrate quotations into essays. Note:

- the punctuation used to introduce the quotations.
- where the quotation marks begin and end.
- if the quotation begins with a capital letter.

(The citation in parentheses after the quote is covered in Part 3).

1. Briefly introduce the quotation with a phrase.
    - Place a comma after the phrase that introduces the quotation.
    - Begin the quote with a capital letter.

Example:

Although the United Nations is firmly committed to creating a world society built on peace and harmony, it has never been naive about how peace might have to be achieved. The very first lines of Chapter 1 in ***The Charter of the United Nations*** clearly state, "To maintain international peace and security, and to that end: to take effective collective measures for the prevention and removal of threats to the peace, and for the suppression of acts of aggression or other breaches of the peace" (United Nations, 1945, p. 3). These principles of removing threats and stopping aggressive acts suggest that violence may be a necessary means to achieve the goal of a peaceful and secure world.

2. Introduce the quotation with a complete sentence that states its significance to the essay's thesis.
   - Place a colon at the end of the complete sentences that introduces the quotation.
   - Begin the quote with a capital letter.

Example:

> Although the United Nations is firmly committed to creating a world society built on peace and harmony, it has never been naive about how peace might have to be achieved. The very first lines of Chapter 1 in ***The Charter of the United Nations*** clearly state that violence may sometimes be necessary to achieve a higher ideal: "To maintain international peace and security, and to that end: to take effective collective measures for the prevention and removal of threats to the peace, and for the suppression of acts of aggression or other breaches of the peace" (United Nations, 1945, p. 3). These principles of removing threats and stopping aggressive acts leave open the option of military force to maintain a peaceful and secure world.

3. Blend the quotation directly into the essay writer's sentence.
   - No punctuation is necessary if the quotation is blended into a sentence using a word such as *that*.
   - Begin the quote with a lowercase letter.

Example:

> The very first lines of Chapter 1 in ***The Charter of the United Nations*** clearly state that "to maintain international peace and security, and to that end: to take effective collective measures for the prevention and removal of threats to the peace, and for the suppression of acts of aggression or other breaches of the peace" (United Nations, 1945, p. 3).

4. Place the introductory phrase inside the quote.
   - Use commas to separate the quote from the introductory phrase.

Example:

> "To maintain international peace and security," are the first words of Chapter 1 in ***The Charter of the United Nations***, but the text immediately continues, "and to that end: to take effective collective measures for the prevention and removal of threats to the peace, and for the suppression of acts of aggression or other breaches of the peace" (United Nations, 1945, p. 3).

5. If a quotation is more than about 40 words, do not use quotation marks.
   - End the sentence before the quote with a colon, start the quotation on the next line, and indent it.
   - Restart the paragraph on a new line after the quotation:

Example:

Indent →

Restart paragraph →

> Although the United Nations is firmly committed to creating a world society built on peace and harmony, it has never been naive about how peace might have to be achieved. The very first lines of Chapter 1 in ***The Charter of the United Nations*** clearly state:
>
> > To maintain international peace and security, and to that end: to take effective collective measures for the prevention and removal of threats to the peace, and for the suppression of acts of aggression or other breaches of the peace, and to bring about by peaceful means, and in conformity with the principles of justice and international law, adjustment or settlement of international disputes or situations which might lead to a breach of the peace (United Nations, 1945, p. 3).
>
> These principles of removing threats and stopping aggressive acts leave open the option of military force to maintain a peaceful and secure world.

Exercise 8

Correct the errors with the use of quotations in the following passages. Rewrite the passages if necessary.

1. "In China, India, Indonesia and Korea, American, British, Dutch and French Imperialism, based on the concept of the supremacy of Europeans over Asians, has been completely and perfectly exploded. In Malaya and Indo-China British and French imperialisms are being shaken to their foundations by powerful and revolutionary national liberation movements." In his 1953 speech "No Easy Road to Freedom," Nelson Mandela referred to successful movements around the world to inspire similar change in Africa.

2. In *Civilization and Its Discontents*, Freud (1930) asserted that "The liberty of the individual is no gift of civilization. It was greatest before there was any civilization," but admitted: "though then, it is true, it had for the most part no value, since the individual was scarcely in a position to defend it." (p. 42).

Part 3 Citing sources

Section 1 Citation components and integration

The source of every paraphrase, summary, and quotation must be identified in the essay. This is called citation (or referencing). Citation is necessary to:

- indicate the origin of ideas.
- allow readers to find the original source.
- avoid plagiarism.

NOTE: If source information is included in an essay without citation, it is plagiarism.

Citation has two equally important components:

- a References list on a separate page at the end of the essay, which alphabetically lists all the sources used in the essay.
- in-text (or parenthetical) citation used in the essay paragraphs.

All citation examples in this textbook follow the American Psychological Association (APA) style.

1. References

Every source used in an essay must appear in the References list. APA requires that each source be entered on the list in a certain way depending on the type of source, such as a book, a journal article, a newspaper article, or information from the internet. Refer to official APA resources for complete style rules and guidelines.

In general, two things are required for in-text citation:

- whatever information is written first for a source on the References list (usually the name of the author).
- the year the source was published.

For example, this is a journal article entry on a References list:

Giordano, P. (2012). The trendy Asian tigers. *Fashion Business Quarterly Review*, *12*(2), 25–29.

When information from this source appears in the essay, Giordano (the first piece of information listed) and 2012 (the publication year of the source) must appear in the essay to make in-text citation.

2. In-text citation

There are three patterns of in-text citation.

Pattern 1:

information from the source + (last name of author, + year published in parentheses) + final punctuation

Example:

The fashion industry continues to enjoy growing profits due to the Asian consumers' love affair with brand name goods. The Japanese market alone constitutes over a third of total worldwide sales of Vuitton, Prada, and Gucci products, and the increasing demand for high-end fashion in China and South Korea is expected to account for almost 50% of the projected growth in the industry over the next decade (Giordano, 2012).

In Pattern 1, both the author's name and publication year (Giordano, 2012) indicate that the information before the parenthesis came from a source. If the reader wished to check the source, he or she could refer to the References page, find the author's last name, and find the complete information for the source.

Using this pattern suggests:

- the source details are basic or uncontroversial facts.
- the information is more useful to the reader than the author's name and year of publication.

Pattern 2:

author's name in sentence text + (year published in parentheses) + information from the source

Example:

The fashion industry continues to enjoy growing profits due to the Asian consumers' love affair with brand name goods. Giordano (2012) reports that the Japanese market alone constitutes over a third of total worldwide sales of Vuitton, Prada, and Gucci products, and the increasing demand for high-end fashion in China and South Korea is expected to account for almost 50% of the projected growth in the industry over the next decade.

In Pattern 2, the author's name is integrated into the text of the essay before the source's information. Only the publication year is put in parentheses (2012) and placed directly after the author's name.

Using this pattern:

- draws attention to the author and year of publication because these may be important. The author may be a recognized expert in the field, or having recent information may be significant to the topic.
- allows the essay writer to show the author's position on or attitude towards the source information (see Part 4, Using reporting verbs and phrases).

Pattern 3:

year published in sentence text + author's name in sentence text + information from the source

In a 2012 Fashion Business Quarterly Review *article, Giordano states that the fashion industry continues to enjoy growing profits due to the Asian consumers' love affair with brand name goods. The Japanese market alone constitutes over a third of total worldwide sales of Vuitton, Prada, and Gucci products, and the increasing demand for high-end fashion in China and South Korea is expected to account for almost 50% of the projected growth in the industry over the next decade.*

In Pattern 3, both the publication year and the author's name are integrated into the text of the essay before the source information. When this happens, parentheses are not necessary.

Using this pattern has similar effects as Pattern 2, but in addition:

- the publication year is given greater importance.

In-text citations can be modified in several different ways depending on the type and details of each source. See Appendix B for a list of possible ways to modify in-text citation.

Exercise 1

Look at the in-text citation of the model essay about tourism in Antarctica on pages 53–59 and number them 1 to 21:

- Match each in-text citation to its entry in the References list and write the number next to the entry.
- Then below, write the number of the in-text citation where:

1. two sources are to support one point. Explain how they appear.
2. "et al." is used. Explain why this is used.
3. "as cited in" is used. Explain why this is used.
4. "and" is changed to "&" in some sources. Explain why it changes.
5. the page number of the source information appears. Explain why it is used.
6. The letters "a" and "b" have been added after the publication dates in-text and on the References list. Explain why they are used.

Section 2 Common knowledge

It is not necessary to cite source information that is considered common knowledge. Generally, information is considered common knowledge if it is:

- accepted as universally true or factual.
- not doubted or arguable.
- unlikely to change.

For example, the following fact does not require citation:
The rules defining modern football were drawn up in England by the Football Association in 1863.

Although the essay reader may not know about the history of football, checking several other sources would show exactly the same information.

The following are normally regarded as common knowledge:

- Historical facts:
  The Treaty of Versailles was signed in 1919.
- Geographic facts:
  Portugal, Spain, Andorra, and Gibraltar comprise the Iberian Peninsula.
- Established facts:
  The Indian city of Mumbai was once known as Bombay.
- Basic scientific facts:
  Water boils at 100° C and freezes at 0° C under normal conditions.

The majority of researched information used in an academic essay is original ideas, theories, interpretations, statistics, research findings, and reports. This information is not considered common knowledge and therefore needs citation.

NOTE: If you are unsure about whether information is common knowledge or not, the best strategy is to use citation to avoid plagiarism.

Exercise 2

Which of the following details would have to be cited if used in an academic essay?

1. Throughout history, thousands of animal species have become extinct.
2. Of the millions killed in war in the twentieth century, an estimated 75% were innocent women and children.
3. The area of volcanic activity around the Pacific Ocean is commonly referred to as the Ring of Fire.
4. From 1994 to 1998, reported natural disasters averaged 428 per year, but from 1999 to 2003, this figure shot up by two-thirds to an average of 707 natural disasters each year.

5. At an estimated 0.78 children per woman in 2012, Singapore's fertility rate is the lowest in the world and far below the 2.1 needed to maintain the population.

6. The six principal organizations of the United Nations are the General Assembly, Security Council, Economic and Social Council, Trusteeship Council, International Court of Justice, and Secretariat.

7. Given the tigers' current rate of population decline, many biologists predict that it will become extinct in the wild in fifteen to twenty years.

8. Founded in 1088, the University of Bologna is widely regarded as the oldest university in the world.

9. Despite having religious aspects like ideas on an afterlife, Confucianism is not widely seen as a religion because it does not have core beliefs on the nature of the human soul.

10. According to several prominent NGOs, government corruption is the most significant obstacle to poverty relief in developing countries.

Part 4

Using reporting verbs and phrases

Reporting verbs are necessary to:

- accurately report the source author's position on or attitude towards the information.
- help express the significance of an idea or evidence.
- critically evaluate source information.

Section 1 Using reporting verbs

Below are some of the most common reporting verbs. Using reporting verbs often follows three general grammatical patterns:

Pattern 1:

writer + reporting verb + **that** + subject + verb

acknowledge	discover	point out
agree	doubt	predict
appear	estimate	prove
argue	explain	recommend
assert	find	report
believe	imply	reveal
claim	indicate	show
conclude	insist	state
contend	maintain	suggest
demonstrate	note	write
determine	observe	

Example:

Researchers ***have demonstrated that*** *the food additive is harmful to children.*

Pattern 1 verbs may also appear in a subordinate clause beginning with *as* and followed by a comma:

Example:

As *Ellis (2000)* ***insists,*** *the research conclusions should be viewed cautiously due to the small number of subjects tested.*

Exercise 1

Complete the following sentences with an appropriate Pattern 1 reporting verb.

1. Environmentalists ____________ chemicals had seeped into the water table (Baxter, 2007).

2. As researchers ____________, the new procedure is environmentally safe (Wu et al., 2002).

3. This evidence ____________ lowering the legal drinking age creates a greater sense of responsibility among young people and could reduce rates of alcohol abuse.

Pattern 2:

writer + reporting verb + somebody/something + **for** + noun/gerund

account	criticize	single out
applaud	emphasize	stress
blame	praise	
condemn	recognize	

Example:

Marx (1859) actually ***praised*** *the United States* ***for*** *its freedom, which was alien to Europe in the 1800s.*

Exercise 2

Complete the following sentences with an appropriate Pattern 2 reporting verb.

1. Both Bernard (2003) and Kim (2005) ________________ the need **for** more research before drawing any conclusions.

2. A 2001 World Bank report ________________ the Nigerian government **for** its efforts to combat corruption.

3. The prime minister ________________ the media **for** causing public panic over the nuclear accident.

Pattern 3:

writer + reporting verb + somebody/something + **as** + noun/gerund/adjective

appraise	depict	perceive
assess	describe	portray
characterize	dismiss	present
class	evaluate	refer
classify	identify	regard
define	interpret	view

Example:

Although Friedman and Garibaldi (2005) ***present*** *their data* ***as*** *conclusive, they failed to account for all the inconsistencies among the test subjects.*

Exercise 3

Complete the following sentences with an appropriate Pattern 3 reporting verb.

1. Researchers ________________ gambling addicts as "being guided by unbounded irrationality" (Huet & Unger, 2001, p. 103).

2. O'Leary (1998) ________________ the removal of banking controls in the 1980s as reckless and warned of future economic problems.

3. Chiang, Faber, and Choi (2011) ________________ the sudden change in policy as a sign of internal turmoil within the government.

Pattern variations:

A) who + **at** + where + **pattern** + informations

Examples:

*Researchers **at** The Center for Disease Control **found that** the virus was highly contagious among laboratory rats (Dolan, Visnicky, Young, & Perez, 2008).*

*Donnie Chen (2012) **at** the Asian Police Alliance **describes** drug traffickers **as** "the greatest threat to public safety" (p. 2) due to their massive arsenal of weapons and increasing willingness to use them.*

B) **In a report issued by/from** + source + (pattern) + information

Examples:

***In a report issued by** the World Bank, the subcommittee on trade **viewed** the modest growth **as** encouraging despite being well below projections.*

***In a report from** the University of Middle Florida, sudden increases in food prices have caused many of those living below the poverty line to reduce the number of daily meals they have from three to two.*

C) **A** + year + source + **report/study** + (pattern) + information

Examples:

***A** 2004 Harvard **study suggests that** drinking coffee may indeed have health benefits (Thomas & van Dyck).*

***A** 2011 British Commission **report criticized** city officials for waiting too long to report the increased bacteria levels in the water.*

D) **According to** + source + (pattern) + information

Examples:

***According to** Li (2010), the genome test results support the substantial body of archeological evidence that concludes rice domestication began in the Yangtze River valley.*

***According to** economists at the East Asia Alliance Fund, the boom in tourism to the island does not account for the dramatic increases in food prices (Bae & Kobayashi, 2009).*

Meaning and strength of reporting verbs

Reporting verbs have different meanings and different levels of strength. It is important to choose a reporting verb that

- accurately matches the meaning of the source information.
- matches the strength of the source author's position or attitude.

Example:

"Despite the well-publicized delays in the final development of the operating system, the new tablet will definitely be released on schedule." (source information taken from a company's homepage)

The following use of reporting verbs would be ineffective:

A. The company explains that the new tablet will be released on time.

B. The company indicates that the new tablet will be released on time.

A is incorrect because the company did not explain anything. **B** is inappropriate because *indicates* is too weak. The company used *definitely* to indicate certainty in its plans, so a stronger verb would more accurately represent this attitude.

The following use of reporting verbs would be effective:

C. The company insists that the new tablet will be released on time.

D. The company maintains that the new tablet will be released on time.

The reporting verbs *insist* and *maintain* both accurately convey the certainty expressed in the source with *will definitely be released on schedule*.

Avoiding neutral reporting verbs

Many reporting verbs, such as *said* and *stated*, express a neutral position and are appropriate when the source author is truly conveying a neutral position. However, these reporting verbs are often overused and result in less accurate and repetitive writing.

Example:

The Asian Police Alliance <u>says</u> the rise in drug trafficking in Asia is because of the influence of Western pop culture through movies and TV shows.

This example would be more accurate if a stronger reporting verb were used:

The Asian Police Alliance <u>blames</u> the rise in drug trafficking in Asia on the influence of Western pop culture through movies and TV shows.

The verb *blames* reflects the police's accusatory attitude regarding Western influence in Asia. Other reporting verbs expressing a similar attitude strongly are *accused*, *criticized*, and *condemned*.

Exercise 4

For each sentence, replace *said* or *stated* with a verb which more accurately reports the meaning, strength, or attitude.

1. A researcher from the South Asian Arranged Marriage Council said that there is no basis for the belief that "love marriages" are more stable than arranged marriages.

   a) estimates b) demands c) insists

2. The school board's president stated that children be required to attend school seven days a week.

   a) recommended b) noted c) confirmed

3. A physicist from the government's military council said that radiation levels in the area of the nuclear accident pose no immediate threat to human health.

   a) predicted b) assured c) proved

4. A report from the World Football Council states that one out of every two children in the world plays or watches soccer.

   a) estimates b) acknowledges c) argues

5. The Association of American Universities said that tuition increases over the past decade have hurt the ability of many students to attend university.

   a) admitted b) demonstrated c) argued

6. The Union of Flight Attendants stated that any reduction in cabin staffing will compromise safety and comfort, especially on long international flights.

   a) declared b) discovered c) warned

7. Eastern Automobile CEO Chuck Croft said that car travel will eventually become much safer and cleaner than any other form of transportation thanks to new technological developments.

   a) predicted b) doubted c) observed

8. Animal behaviorist Sylvia Fassbender stated that pack animals such as wolves and lions participate in bullying behavior towards those seen as weak in their group.

   a) discovered b) criticized c) illustrated

9. In response to the environmental group's protest, Black Star Oil Corporation says that no harm will come to wildlife if drilling is permitted in protected wetlands.

a) anticipates b) insists c) doubts

10. Professor Faria Khan of Middle Eastern University stated that war is counterproductive when she said, "The best way to fight terrorism is with olive branches."

a) explained b) implied c) determined

UNIT

4

Accuracy and Clarity

Part 1 Hedging and intensifying

Section 1 Using hedging and intensifying

Hedging and intensifying are essential in academic writing when trying to express information clearly and accurately. Clear and accurate writing makes an essay powerful and persuasive.

Hedging means using words to reduce the certainty of statements. Information and ideas are often not 100% certain: their exact certainty is often unknown, cannot be known, or is not important. Hedging allows essay writers to express information and ideas like these as accurately as possible.

Examples:

Original statement:

Therefore, unfair trade practices are the source of conflicts over globalization.

Hedged statement:

*Therefore, unfair trade practices are **often** the source of conflicts over globalization.*

The original statement is an over-generalization: It cannot be known that "unfair trade practices" are the only cause of conflicts over globalization. Adding the hedging word *often* makes the statement more accurate.

Original statement:

The increase in the number of Western-style cafés in Asia means Asian consumers are more accepting of Western influences.

Hedged statement:

*The increase in the number of Western-style cafés in Asia **may** mean Asian consumers are more accepting of Western influences.*

In the original statement, the increase in Western-style cafés is insufficient evidence to make the conclusion about Asian consumers. Adding the hedging word *may* makes the statement more believable.

Intensifying means using words to increase the certainty of statements. Using intensifying words helps show the power and significance of certain information and ideas. However, intensifying must still represent information and ideas accurately.

Examples:

Original statement:

Shanahan (2011) reports that the rise in unemployment in the United States is attributable to the outsourcing of jobs to countries which provide cheaper labor.

Intensified statement:

*Shanahan (2011) reports that the rise in unemployment in the United States is **directly** attributable to the outsourcing of jobs to countries which provide cheaper labor.*

The intensified statement uses the word *directly* to emphasize the significance of outsourced labor as being a major cause of unemployment.

Original statement:

The development of anesthesia in the early twentieth century was a first step in allowing doctors to perform more complex surgeries.

Intensified statement:

*The development of anesthesia in the early twentieth century was an **important** first step in allowing doctors to perform more complex surgeries.*

The intensified statement uses the word *important* to emphasize the significance of anesthesia in medicine.

Section 2 Vocabulary for hedging and intensifying

Vocabulary that can be used for hedging and intensifying is listed below.

Hedging		Intensifying
• appear • assume • imply • seem • suggest • tend to	Verbs	• argue • assert • contend • demand • insist
• can • could • may • might	Modal verbs	• do • have to • must • will • would
• about • approximate • conceivable • few • many • most • often • partial • possible • rare • relative • similar • some • sometimes • somewhat	Adjectives	• absolute • all • certain • clear • complete • definite • dramatic • entire • essential • high • important • most • obvious • quite • sharp • significant • specific • strong • sudden • thorough • vast • very • whole
• approximately • conceivably • likely • likely • partially • perhaps • possibly • probably • rarely • relatively • usually	Adverbs	• absolutely • always • certainly • clearly • completely • definitely • entirely • essentially • highly • indeed • in fact • largely • most (importantly) • obviously • sharply • significantly • specifically • strongly • undoubtedly • vastly • wholly • widely

Many of these words can also be used in conjunction with each other to modify meaning.

Examples:

Hedged

Intensified

The findings ***seem to indicate*** *that the virus can be spread through physical contact.*

The findings ***indicate*** *that the virus can be spread through physical contact.*

The findings ***clearly indicate*** *that the virus can be spread through physical contact.*

Exercise 1

Read the following paragraph, and underline the words that hedge or intensify.

The globalization of industrial agriculture has also failed to provide the promised economic benefits to Central American farmers. In order to compete in global trade, many farmers have turned to monoculture, growing only one crop rather than multiple crops, to maximize yields. Statistics from the World Currency Group (2008) suggest that this change in agricultural practice has likely contributed to a reduction in rural unemployment throughout Central America by about 4% since 2001. Although the change to specialized, high-demand export crops may account for this decrease, employment figures alone cannot definitively show that the situation has improved. In fact, other economic indicators appear to negate the importance of the employment numbers. Recent figures from the Central American Agribusiness Association (2011) clearly indicate that real income levels during the same time period also decreased. It may be possible to conclude, therefore, that while monoculture can increase the demand for labor, its higher yields tend to reduce the global market value of the crop, lower profits for farmers, and maintain poverty in the region.

Exercise 2

Change the following intensified sentences into hedged sentences. Use different hedging words in each.

Example:

Obviously, television is a **far** more effective educational tool than books.

➔ Television **may** be a more effective educational tool than books.

1. Research clearly shows that children are much better second language learners than adults.

 ____

 ____

2. Analysts completely agree that the United Nations has successfully intervened in regional armed conflicts all around the world.

 ____

 ____

3. All teenagers definitely consider social networking sites an essential part of their friendship experiences.

 ____

 ____

4. It is obvious that the international appeal of the Hollywood film industry is solely due to its financial and technical power.

 ____

 ____

5. Scientists insist that global warming will be the most catastrophic event in human history.

____

____

Exercise 3

Change the following hedged sentences into intensified sentences. Use different intensifying words in each.

Example:

Although they **may** increase overall travel time, airport security checks **appear** to be necessary for safeguarding air travel.

➔ Although they **do** increase overall travel time, airport security checks are **essential** for safeguarding air travel.

1. The fashion industry might be one area in which it is important that models have good looks.

____

____

2. In some cases, animal rights organizations tend to say that animals should not be used in experiments.

____

____

3. Medical evidence seems to suggest that regular cardiovascular exercise will probably help reduce the chance of heart disease.

____

____

4. A degree of familiarity with computer technology could be useful for some administrative office jobs.

____

____

5. After earthquakes, trained sniffer dogs can play a role in finding a few survivors buried under collapsed buildings.

____

____

Exercise 4

Rewrite the sentences to hedge or intensify their meaning.

Example:

Siddiqui says that while the global food supply is sufficient, its unequal distribution is the cause of hunger.

→ Siddiqui states that while the global food supply is sufficient, its unequal distribution is **one of the** causes of hunger. (hedged answer)

→ Siddiqui **asserts** that while the global food supply is **indeed** sufficient, its unequal distribution is the **main** cause of hunger. (intensified answer)

1. Kovacs (2012) says that developing countries benefit from removing restrictions on trade.

   ____

   ____

2. Globalization leads to the "Englishization" of the world as people need to speak English to participate in the global economy.

   ____

   ____

3. Corruption is a problem in developing countries, but Sanchez (2010) says it is also a problem in developed countries.

   ____

   ____

4. New medicines are available in developed countries, but they are not available in developing parts of the world.

   ____

   ____

5. Environmental degradation in the developing world is not caused by the indigenous people, but by multinational companies in industrial countries taking their natural resources.

   ____

   ____

Part

2 Academic sentence styles

Section 1 Conjunctions

The relationship between ideas within and between sentences must be clear for writing to be coherent and powerful. This requires the proper use of transitional words and phrases to express these relationships.

Conjunctions are essential words that create the complex sentences required in academic writing.

1. Coordinating conjunctions

Coordinating conjunctions link parts of compound sentences using these prepositions: *for, and, nor, but, or, yet, so.*

These conjunctions:

- show a relationship between independent clauses, phrases, and words in the same sentence.
- suggest that the information joined in the sentence is equally important.

A comma is needed before the coordinating conjunction if it is followed by a full clause:

Many people have a preference for a certain alcohol, ***but*** *beer consumption tends to increase overall during periods of economic growth.*

No comma is needed if the coordinating conjunction joins two nouns, verbs, or other word form:

Professor Nate Nakamura researched ***and*** *developed ways to clone farm animals, such as sheep* ***and*** *chickens,* ***yet*** *he has been the target of protests by various religious* ***and*** *animal rights groups for the ethics behind such science.*

Martin Luther King, Jr., spoke eloquently ***yet*** *powerfully, which made him the ideal spokesperson for the American civil rights movement.*

NOTE: A **serial comma** is a comma placed before the last item in a list to ensure the item is not connected to the others.

A. *Society's elite prohibited men without property and women from voting or having any kind of political involvement.*

B. *Society's elite prohibited men without property, and women from voting or having any kind of political involvement.*

Serial comma

Example A implies men had to own property and own women. Example B makes it clear there were two separate groups who could not vote or have any political involvement: men without property in one group, and women in the other.

In general, try to avoid beginning sentences with a coordinating conjunction. One exception, however, is when trying to emphasize the relationship information or an idea has with the sentence preceding it:

The prime minister invested heavily in his attempt to be re-elected. ***But*** *he failed.*

Writing "he failed" as a separate sentence and using the contrasting word "but" emphasizes the point more powerfully.

2. Correlative conjunctions

The correlative conjunctions are *both … and, not only … but also, just as … so, either … or, neither … nor, whether … or.*

These conjunctions:

- join information of equal importance.
- add emphasis to the joined information.

Compare the following sentences:

A. *Mozart* ***and*** *Beethoven enjoyed great success and fame during their own lifetimes.*

B. ***Both*** *Mozart* ***and*** *Beethoven enjoyed great success and fame during their own lifetimes.*

In example B, the word "both" emphasizes the two subjects' equal relationship more than in sentence A.

3. Subordinating conjunctions

Subordinating conjunctions can indicate several different relationships. They:

- create a subordinate clause that depends on an independent clause to express a complete idea.
- suggest that the independent main clause is more importance than the dependent subordinate clause.

Below is a table of their common functions with examples.

Showing opposition and contrast	although even though though whereas while	• ***Although*** *many heads of terrorist groups have been killed or captured in the past year, suicide attacks have actually increased over the same period.*
Introducing an alternative	if unless	• *Soccer will likely continue to be a fringe sport in the United States* ***unless*** *there is some way to make the games more exciting to watch.*
Showing chronological order or a sequence	after as as soon as before since until when while	• ***As soon as*** *the police descended on the protestors, the peaceful demonstration quickly turned into an uncontrollable riot.* • ***Before*** *the expansion and adoption of social networking on the internet, keeping in touch with people took a lot of time and money.*
Showing cause and effect	as because since	• ***Since*** *the Board of Education began emphasizing conversational skills over grammar knowledge, students' English proficiency has improved significantly.*

A subordinating conjunction:

- can begin a sentence or be used between the clauses.
- needs a comma between the clauses if the dependent clause comes first.
- does not need a comma if the independent clause comes first.

Examples:

Even though *the government distributed it to hospitals and clinics, the vaccine was known to be completely ineffective in treating the virus.*

The vaccine was known to be completely ineffective in treating the virus ***even though*** *the government distributed it to hospitals and clinics.*

4. Subjunctive adverbs

Subjunctive adverbs show a relationship between ideas in different sentences. Below are the common functions of subjunctive adverbs, with examples.

The idea is a logical conclusion from the previous idea.	accordingly consequently hence subsequently therefore thus	• *Police work often requires strenuous physical activity.* ***Accordingly****, entry requirements for many police forces include physical health and fitness criteria.* • *Studies indicate that children who attend inner-city schools have fewer educational opportunities compared with the national average.* ***Hence****, these children are under-represented in jobs which require high academic qualifications.*
The idea contrasts with the previous idea.	conversely however in contrast instead nevertheless nonetheless still	• *Police work often requires strenuous physical activity.* ***Conversely****, office work may be detrimental to overall health as it requires very little movement.* • *Studies indicate that children who attend inner-city schools have fewer educational opportunities compared with the national average.* ***Nonetheless****, every year a number of these children are selected for places in top-ranked universities.*
The idea supports the previous idea.	additionally also for example for instance furthermore indeed likewise moreover similarly to illustrate	• *Police work often requires strenuous physical activity.* ***Furthermore****, the job may also put officers in dangerous situations.* • *Studies indicate that children who attend inner-city schools have fewer educational opportunities compared with the national average.* ***Indeed****, parents of children in these schools may be justified in claiming that the educational system is unfair.*

A subjunctive adverb:

- can often be placed at the beginning, after the main subject, or at the end of the sentence.
- needs commas to separate it from the words around it.

Examples:

Henry Ford neither invented the car nor the production line. ***However,*** *he was the first to mass-produce such a sophisticated machine efficiently.*

Henry Ford neither invented the car nor the production line. He was, ***however,*** *the first to mass-produce such a sophisticated machine efficiently.*

Henry Ford neither invented the car nor the production line. He was the first to mass-produce such a sophisticated machine efficiently, ***however.***

Section 2 Linking ideas with punctuation

1. Semi-colons (;)

When the relationship between ideas is obvious, semi-colons:

- can replace a conjunction between two independent clauses.
- emphasize the close relationship between the ideas.

Study the following examples.

Coordinating conjunction:
The North American black bear population remains strong, ***but*** *the Asian black bear population is decreasing.*

Subordinating conjunction:
The North American black bear population remains strong, ***whereas*** *the Asian black bear population is decreasing.*

Subjunctive adverb:
The North American black bear population remains strong. ***However,*** *the Asian black bear population is decreasing.*

Semi-colon:
The North American black bear population remains strong; the Asian black bear population is decreasing.

2. Colons (:)

Colons join an independent clause to a word, phrase, or clause that exemplifies or explains the preceding idea:
In most countries around the world, people routinely and legally use three of the most addictive drugs: ***alcohol, nicotine, and caffeine.***

In the example, the list after the colon specifies the three drugs introduced in the preceding clause as "three of the most addictive drugs."

If an independent clause follows the colon, start it with a capital letter:
Cultures which have an indigenous tradition of vampires or vampire-like creatures normally have one crucial practice in common: ***They bury their dead rather than cremating them.***

In this example, the independent clause after the colon begins with a capital letter and explains the "one crucial practice in common" stated in the first clause.

Exercise 1

Using appropriate conjunctions, a semicolon, or a colon, write several possible sentences using the information given.

Example:

- 1946 scientists realize DNA could be transferred between organisms – possible to create genetically modified (GM) food
- 1983 first genetically modified plant – tobacco

Possible answer sentences:

Although the idea of genetically modifying (GM) organisms dates from 1946, it was not until 1983 when the first commercial GM crops appeared.

Scientists realized that DNA could be transferred between organisms, but it was not until 1983 that the first GM crop was created.

Scientists realized that DNA could be transferred between organisms. However, it was not until 1983 that the first GM crop was created.

In 1946, scientists realized that DNA could be transferred to other organisms to genetically modify them. But it took until 1983 to create the first GM crop: tobacco.

1.

- historians disagree on Native American population before European colonization
- some estimate low 30 million – others high 60 million

____

____

____

____

2.

- Sony – market value of $21 billion
- Samsung – market value of $162 billion

____

____

____

____

3.

- the word "snake" from proto Indo-European word "snag" – "to crawl, or creep"
- the word "sneak" same origin

____

____

____

____

4.

- Kenya coffee considered best in the world – noted intense flavor, full body, and mild aroma.
- not large companies with production – about 70% produced on small-scale farms

____

____

____

____

5.

- 2010 statistics – rapid increase – read newspapers on internet
- 1.9 billion online newspaper readers worldwide

____

____

____

____

Section 3 Sentences in context

The order of information in a sentence is often determined by the sentences around it. Sentences must logically connect with each other to create paragraph cohesion, so writers must decide where to best place information to clearly indicate important points and achieve smooth transitions between sentences.

Examples:

A. *Beethoven enjoyed widespread fame as a composer during his own lifetime,* ***but*** *Bach was only known regionally as a talented musician during his. Beethoven* ***and*** *Bach are now widely considered among the most important composers of classical music in history.*

In example A, the first sentence shows a contrasting relationship between Beethoven and Bach using "but." In the next sentence, however, the coordinating conjunction "and" shows Bach and Beethoven's relationship to be similar. This may confuse the reader.

B. *Beethoven enjoyed widespread fame as a composer during his own lifetime,* ***but*** *Bach was only known regionally as a talented musician during his.* ***However, both*** *Beethoven* ***and*** *Bach are now widely considered among the most important composers of classical music in history.*

In example B, the writer uses "however" to indicate a contrasting relationship between the sentences, and then uses "both ... and" to emphasize that Beethoven and Bach share an important characteristic. This wording helps emphasize the idea that Bach eventually achieved a similar level of notoriety as Beethoven.

C. ***Although*** *the public is overwhelmingly against child labor, there are still many factories in developing countries which employ children younger than 10 years old.* ***Because*** *the general public purchases the products produced by these factories, factories continue to use cheap child labor.*

D. ***Although*** *the public is overwhelmingly against child labor, there are still many factories in developing countries which employ children younger than 10 years old. Factories continue to use cheap child labor* ***because*** *the general public purchases the products produced by these factories.*

The first sentence in both C and D describes factories. However, the second sentence in example C starts with information about the general public, which is an abrupt transition to a new idea which has not been mentioned yet. In contrast, the second sentence in example D starts with information which has already been introduced in the previous sentence. This is a smooth transition because the reader expects the same idea to be continued.

Exercise 2 **Use the information in the bullet points to write a sentence that logically connects to the sentence provided.**

Example:

- 2000 first food crop golden rice
- nutrient value increased

Although the idea of genetically modifying (GM) organisms dates from 1946, it was not until 1983 when the first commercial GM crop, tobacco, appeared.

Possible answer sentence:

Furthermore, it was not until 2000 when the first food crop, golden rice, was genetically modified to have increased nutrients.

1.
   - argue over population killed by European diseases
   - some estimates 40% some 80%

Historians argue over the Native American population level before European colonization: some estimates are as low as 30 million and others as high as 60 million.

____

____

2.
   - *Forbes* magazine (2011), biggest public companies: Samsung = 26th, Sony = 477th

Although Sony is valued at $21 billion, Samsung is almost eight times larger at $162 billion.

____

____

3.
   - the word "snail"
   - same origin

Both the word "snake" and "sneak" come from the same proto Indo-European word "snag," meaning "to crawl, or creep."

____

____

4.

- Kenya tea – intense full body, malty flavor
- mainly small-scale farms produced

Kenyan coffee is noted for its intense flavor, full body, and mild aroma and is rarely produced by large companies, with about 70% produced on small-scale farms.

____

____

5.

- traditional newspapers – slight increase
- still 2.3 billion read each day

According to 2010 figures, the number of people reading newspapers online increased rapidly, and now stands at 1.9 billion readers each day.

____

____

Section 4 Active, passive, and nominalization

When constructing a sentence, writers must decide whether to use an active sentence, a passive sentence, or a nominalization (where an action is represented in noun form). The decision depends on what information in the sentence is important.

In general, active sentences are the most common type of sentence. They represent the relationship between the action and the agent (the noun that performs the action) as clearly as possible. Passive sentences and nominalizations are appropriate when the writer wants to emphasize something other than the agent.

1. Passive sentences

In general, passive sentences are useful in the following situations.

- When the agent is unknown to the reader:
  One of the most valuable paintings in the museum was stolen.
- When the agent is clear to the reader:
  Much of the world's coffee is grown in Brazil.
  The politician was arrested on charges of corruption.
- When the object is more important than the agent:
  Although an internet-like system was first used in 1969, the general public did not use it widely until the 1990s.

  If the writer wants to emphasize the use of the internet rather than who first used it, a passive sentence is more effective.

The new cancer drug was given to patients, and test results were taken.

The writer wants to emphasize the drug and the results rather than the people who conducted the research.

2. Nominalization

Nominalization is common in academic writing because it creates an impersonal and objective tone. It is useful in the following situations.

- **The action is more important than the agent of the action.**

If the writer wants to focus on the issue of drug addiction rather than people who use drugs, a nominalization is more effective:

People may commit crimes because they are addicted to drugs.
➔ *Drug **addiction** may be a cause of crime.*

Nomilization is appropriate if the writer wants to emphasize the action of speeding itself rather than the people who do it:

A recent report into road safety found that people who drive too fast was the primary cause of accidents.
➔ *A recent report into road safety found that **speeding** was the primary cause of accidents.*

- **To be succinct**

Compare these two extracts from an essay on how to boost efficiency among company employees:

A. *Several companies decided to experiment with a new policy allowing their employees to work from home so <u>they can be more productive</u>. However, these companies realized that trying to get employees to <u>be more productive</u> while <u>they work at home is difficult</u> because they <u>become distracted</u> by many things in the home, such as the television or bed.*

B. *<u>To boost productivity</u>, several companies decided to experiment with a new policy allowing their employees to work from home. However, the <u>difficulty</u> of increasing <u>productivity</u> while <u>working from home</u> became apparent as there are many <u>distractions</u> in the home, such as the television or bed.*

Example A uses the active form, which causes the agent (the companies, employees, they) to be mentioned multiple times unnecessarily. The nominalizations in example B make the text more succinct and easier to read.

- **To create coherence**

A verb used in one sentence can be nominalized when it is the topic in the following sentence. This creates an effective link between the two sentences:

*A recent report into road safety **found** that speeding was the primary cause of accidents. These **findings** suggest that law enforcement agencies and public awareness campaigns are not doing enough to discourage people from driving over the speed limit.*

Exercise 3

Considering the guidelines for using active, passive, and nominalization, choose the most effective sentence to continue.

1. Shakespeare wrote *Hamlet* some time at the start of the seventeenth century.

   a. Performances of *Hamlet* are more common than any other Shakespeare play.

   b. *Hamlet* is performed by theater companies more than any other Shakespeare play.

2. In contrast to most of the public safety committee's reports, the impact of this particular report was ineffective.

   a. Important information was omitted, which caused confusion.

   b. Important information was omitted, which confused people.

3. For the average citizen, it remains difficult to become rich.

   a. Economist Karen Miller claims that the most significant barrier to individual wealth creation is lack of financial incentives.

   b. Economist Karen Miller claims that the most significant barrier to wealth creation is the fact that people have no incentive to create wealth.

4. A 2010 Department of Health survey revealed numerous sources of dissatisfaction with large hospitals.

   a. For example, many people dislike the long waiting times in large hospitals.

   b. For example, waiting times in large hospitals are unpopular.

5. Local people held a meeting in order to identify the key issues affecting quality of life in their neighborhood.

   a. A number of residents said they were afraid to walk alone at night because they were afraid of crime.

   b. A number of residents said they were afraid to walk alone at night because of fear of crime.

6. The intense rivalry between many European soccer clubs means that many players are reluctant to appear in public.

   a. This is because they may be insulted or even attacked by rival fans.

   b. This is because rival fans may insult or even attack them.

Exercise 4

Use the given information to create new active voice, passive voice, and nominalization sentences. Be sure to change the word form and add words so the sentences make sense.

Example:

Subject: researchers
Action verb: collect
Object: data on the behavior of children

Active Voice: Researchers collected data on the behavior of children.
Passive Voice: Data on the behavior of children was collected by researchers.
Nominalization: Collecting data on the behavior of children was the researchers' assignment.

1.

Subject: nuclear watchdog groups
Action verb: investigate
Object: safety of nuclear power plants

Active voice: ______________________

Passive voice: ______________________

Nominalization: ______________________

2.

Subject: political parties
Action verb: survey
Object: citizens' opinions regarding the proposal to increase consumption tax

Active voice: ______________________

Passive voice: ______________________

Nominalization: ______________________

3.

Subject: Ministry of Education
Action verb: examine
Object: how high-speed internet can deliver education more efficiently and effectively

Active voice: ______________________

Passive voice: ______________________

Nominalization: ______________________

4.

Subject:	international human rights organizations
Action verb:	protest
Object:	unequal treatment of women in advanced and developing countries all over the world

Active voice: ______________________________

Passive voice: ______________________________

Nominalization: ______________________________

5.

Subject:	economists
Action verb:	hypothesize
Object:	correlation between the world economic downturn of 2008 and banks being connected by globalization

Active voice: ______________________________

Passive voice: ______________________________

Nominalization: ______________________________

NOTE: For a comprehensive review activity of units 2 and 3, and unit 4 parts 1 and 2, see Appendix C.

Part 3 Editing

All writing, especially the initial drafts, can be improved. Editing is the process of identifying areas for improvement so that the essay is clear and effective. It is a multi-step process which requires the writer to:

1. check effectiveness.
2. check mechanics.
3. have another person check 1 and 2.

Section 1 Checking effectiveness

The first step in editing an essay is to check if the essay effectively does what it is supposed to do – usually to inform and persuade the reader. This requires looking at the information in each paragraph and deciding what should be added, cut, or changed.

To check effectiveness, use the following list of questions and notes for each paragraph type.

1. Introductory paragraph

1. Do the building sentences provide adequate background knowledge on the topic?

   Think of your readers and ask:

   - Is there information which the readers likely already know? If so, cut it from the paragraph.
   - Is any more information needed to help readers understand the essay's thesis? If so, add it to the paragraph.

2. Is the motive for the essay clear?

   Goal: To have readers understand why the essay is worth writing.

3. Does the thesis have a clear position?

   Goal: To have readers understand what the purpose of the essay is.

4. Does the thesis answer the question prompt?

   To answer this question:

   - Look at the essay prompt again.
   - Then look at the thesis.
   - Make sure the thesis uses the words (the same or synonyms) used in the question prompt.

2. Body paragraphs

1. Does each paragraph have a topic sentence which explains the theme of the paragraph?

   Goal: To have readers know what information will be presented in the paragraph.

2. Does each topic sentence directly support the thesis?

   - List all the topic sentences below the thesis.

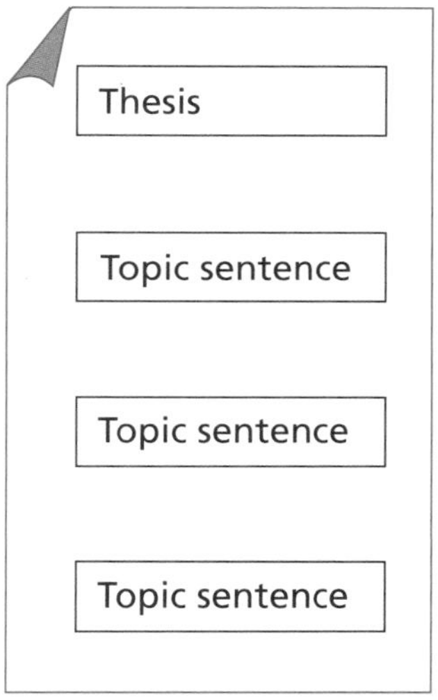

   - Check that there is logical coherence between the thesis and topic sentences.

3. Do the supporting sentences in each body paragraph directly and adequately support the topic sentence?

   Check for the "waltz":

   - Write the number "1" next to each claim sentence. Check that each claim makes a statement in support of the topic sentence.
   - Write the number "2" next to each piece of evidence supporting a claim. Check that:
     - each claim has evidence supporting it.
     - the evidence is directly related to the claim.
   - Write the number "3" next to each explanation sentence. Check that the explanation:
     - helps readers understand the meaning of the evidence in relation to the topic sentence.
     - does not simply repeat the claim.

- If any of the three "waltz" sentences are missing, add them to the paragraph.

4. If the essay requires counter-arguments and rebuttals, are they included?
   Goal: To show that the writer has considered different perspectives.

5. Are the arguments logical?
   Check for:
   - overgeneralizations.
   - irrelevance.

3. Concluding paragraph

1. Are the readers reminded of the thesis and main arguments?
   Check that:
   - the thesis is restated in words different from the original.
   - a summary of each body paragraph is provided.

2. Is there an effective final thought?
   Check that:
   - the essay closes with something for the reader to consider regarding the topic.
   - no new information is provided which may confuse the reader.

Section 2 Checking mechanics

After checking effectiveness, check the mechanics of the essay. This includes:
1. language.
2. use of outside sources.
3. grammar, punctuation, spelling, capitalization.

1. Language

The following questions can be asked to check for clarity, accuracy, and power.

1. Is the meaning of each sentence clear?
   Goal: To ensure each sentence is understandable.

2. Could hedging language be added?
   Goal: To avoid overgeneralizations.

3. Could intensifying language be added?
   Goal: To better emphasize an idea.

4. Are transitional words or phrases necessary?
   Goal: To create cohesion between the sentences.

5. Could the passive form or nominalization be used?
   Goal: To place emphasize on a certain point within a sentence.

6. Is there any redundancy?
   Check that words and sentences are not a repeat of prior words and sentences in the essay. For example:

   Before the early twentieth century, medicines were developed and sold to the public relatively free of government regulations, at times resulting in lethal ~~and deadly~~ consequences ~~which killed many people~~.

   High unemployment causes anxiety in society and is one of the major reasons politicians lose elections. ~~Some politicians are voted out of office because of the public's worry over not being able to find work.~~ Statistics show that less than 10 percent of presidents of a country with an unemployment rate of over 20 percent were re-elected.

7. Are there any first- and second-person pronouns (*I*, *we*, *us*, *you*)?
   The use of such pronouns is not academic style and should be avoided.

2. Use of outside sources

Including information from outside sources is necessary to strengthen arguments in an essay. Therefore, citing sources accurately is essential, so ask the following questions.

1. Is information from outside sources cited properly?
   Goal: To allow readers to find the source of the information easily in the References list.

2. Is plagiarism avoided?
   In addition to proper citation, writers should check that:
   - shorter quotes have quotation marks, longer quotes are indented within a paragraph.
   - paraphrases and summaries do not repeat the wording of the original source.

3. Are quotations overused?
   If so, change some of the quotations to paraphrases or summaries.
   Goal: To have the essay mostly be the writer's own words.

3. Grammar, punctuation, spelling, capitalization

Have the small mistakes been fixed?

Writing filled with errors in grammar, punctuation, spelling, and capitalization is very distracting to a reader. Word processors can identify many of these errors, so writers should fix them before submitting an essay for evaluation. Not doing so reflects poorly on the writer, who could be perceived as lazy for not bothering to correct small mistakes.

NOTE: Certain mistakes are difficult to detect by a word processor, so some time should still be spent manually checking for grammar, punctuation, spelling, and capitalization errors.

Section 3 Editing by another person

After spending time writing and editing an essay, detecting areas for improvement becomes much more difficult for the writer. Therefore, another person's perspective on an essay is helpful because it is fresher and often more objective than the writer's own. Certain errors, such as logical fallacies and confusing wording, are often much easier for another person to detect.

The following checklists are for a two-person editing process. Next to the questions in each step are two boxes, one to be checked by the writer and another one to be checked by an outside person.

First edit: checking effectiveness	Writer	Other
Introductory paragraph		
1. Do the building sentences provide adequate background knowledge on the topic?		
2. Is the motive for the essay clear?		
3. Does the thesis have a clear position?		
4. Does the thesis answer the question prompt?		
Body paragraphs		
5. Does each paragraph have a topic sentence which explains the theme of the paragraph?		
6. Does each topic sentence directly support the thesis?		
7. Do the supporting sentences in each body paragraph directly and adequately support the topic sentence?		
8. Are counter-arguments presented and rebutted?		
9. Are the arguments logical?		
Concluding paragraph		
10. Are the readers reminded of the thesis and main arguments?		
11. Is there an effective final thought?		

Second edit: checking mechanics	Writer	Other
Language		
1. Is the meaning of each sentence clear?		
2. Could hedging language be added?		
3. Could intensifying language be added?		
4. Are transitional words or phrases necessary?		
5. Would the passive voice or nominalization make sentences more effective?		
6. Are there any sentence fragments?		
7. Is there any redundancy?		
8. Is any language subjective?		
9. Are there any first- and second-person pronouns (*I, we, us, you*)?		
Use of outside sources		
10. Is information from outside sources cited properly?		
11. Is plagiarism avoided?		
12. Are quotations overused?		
Grammar, punctuation, spelling, capitalization		
13. Have the small mistakes been fixed?		

Exercise 1

Use the checklists on the previous page and above to edit the following essay.

Essay prompt:

Describe the impact of social networking sites (SNS). Note the similarities and differences in the role SNS plays across different age groups. Include research and statistics to support your arguments.

Social Networking

Many people have used the internet, especially tenagers. Tenager across the Globe are learning how to become internet superstars. In an era of increasing digital connection, social networking sites (SNS) are gaining in popularity and changing the way that generations of internet users communicate with friend and person that they have never met before. More people are using SNS to keep up with people they know and meeting new people. Older genrations claims that SNS interaction is a cheapened or superficial forms of communication and may slow or harm teenagers' ability to grow into young adults who are able to be sociable in society. However, they are wrong because SNS allows them to do many things. For example, mold their identities, broadcast their ideas, and connect with friends both old and new. Some of my friends have even met their spouse through SNS. SNS are excellent because they offer a variety of ways are rewriting the way that teenagers grow as human beings.

SNS allows teenager to mold their identities. Cool sites such as Facbook, which is currently the bigest and best of the SNS, allows users to add a variety of information about themselves to their profiles which can be seen by many people. While all users opt to display basic details such as their gander, birthday and relationship status in their profiles, they also include items such as their favorite books, movies and music (Catherine Dwyer) which help shape their identity even more. Tiffany mentioned, teenagers also feel comfortable displaying their sexual orientation, religion, and political affiliations, and this shows that teenagers are using the SNS experience to help control their overall identity (Tiffany Pempek). Teenagers shape their identity this way and they spend a lot of time on it. This large amount of time teenagers spend shows that they value the attention they get from people who look at their profile. This means they find value face-to-face contact less. It is clear that teenagers spend a lot of time constructing their profile on the internet in SNS. This is a new and better way for teenagers to mold an identity which many people can see.

SNS are changing the way people interact with other people by providing a new form of communication among people. Teenagers are now easily able to broadcast their ideas via one-to-many broadcasting. For instance, it is possible to post messages on a friend's wall through Facebook or share an witty remark with one's followers on Twitter, and these remarks are freely available for other people to see. Twitter is actually more popular than Facebook. SNS are able to have video and photos uploaded. An advantage for teenagers.

Social networking sites gives people who has online access a way to maintain friendships. A person joins a particular SNS because he was invited by a friend. They can stay in touch with friends more easily. Especially with people who live in a foreign country. People can use SNS to find new friends who may share similar interests.

The Twiter network is growing rapidly and always recommends following other users who comment on similar topics (Mashable), so any person who has an account with Twiter can quickly establish connections with individuals who may share similar interests virtually. Facbook allows users to help their contacts find friends on top of the onese they already have through a system which recommends other possible friends. I like how SNS inform me of people I know and which someone else I know knows, and so I can friend these people. It's easy and anyone can realize how SNS can improve their lives by becoming friends with everyone.

In conclusion, through the use of social networking sites, which are constantly developing, tenager are maturing in society faster and quicker than their parents, who are not able to experience the advantages of SNS. Such as establishing their identity or making new friends. Teenagers become smarter because they can exchange opinions with everyone, and having many friends makes teenagers more popular. Research also show that people who do not use SNS have a big disadvantage when trying to find a job. Social networking sites will continue in the future, so it is necessary for teenagers to learn how to interact socially online if they want to be popular and find a job in the fture.

References

Adam Ostrow. "Twitter Starts Offering Personalized Suggestions of Users to Follow." Mashable .com. <http://mashable.com/2010/07/30/twitter-suggestions-for-you/>.

Catherine Dwyer, Starr Roxanne Hiltz and Katia Passerini. "Trust and privacy concern within social networking sites: A comparison of Facebook and MySpace." 2007.

Jilin Chen, et al. 'Make New Friends, but Keep the Old' Recommending People on Social Networking Sites." <http://portal.acm.org/citation.cfm?id=1518701&picked=prox&cfid=3010584&cftoken=38427102>.

Tiffany A. Pempek, Yevdokiya A. Yermolayeva, and Sandra L. Calvert. Journal of Applied Developmental Psychology <http://www.sciencedirect.com/science/>.

Appendix A

Essay genres

The words in the essay prompt indicate what genre of essay is required. Essay genres can usually be divided into three main categories:

1. argumentative essay.
2. expository essay.
3. compare and contrast essay.

An **argumentative** essay takes a position of a controversial issue. For example:

- *Argue for and against extending the school week from five to six days.*
- *How far has the United Nations been successful in fulfilling its stated objectives?*

The writer should include counter-arguments (arguments against his or her position) and rebuttals against the counter-arguments to show that both sides of the issue have been considered thoroughly. The example essay, "Nuclear Power: A viable means of meeting our future energy demands" on page 24 is an argumentative essay.

A common sub-genre of argumentative essays is the **problem-solution** essay. This essay type focuses on a specific problem and proposes a solution. For example:

- *Obesity in children is becoming a serious concern in many developed countries. Suggest a solution to alleviate this problem.*
- *What lifestyle changes can ordinary people make in order to stop global warming?*

The position in the thesis should propose a realistic solution that is supported with clear reasons, details, and examples in the body paragraphs. It is common to include counter-arguments and rebuttals to make the writer's solution more convincing. The example essay on tourism in Antarctica on page 53 is a problem-solution essay.

An **expository** essay explains or describes a system, event, process, or person. For example:

- *Describe the change in the character of Hamlet and account for this change.*
- *Explain how certain twentieth century technology has helped transform the workplace.*

The writer should be conscious of how much readers are likely to know about the topic, and then provide information that may be enlightening to the readers.

A **compare and contrast** essay compares and contrasts specific, related points between two or more subjects. Some essay questions in this genre simply require writers to show the similarities and/or differences between the subjects. For example:

- *Compare the health care systems of France and the United States.*

Other essay questions may require the writer to make an objective evaluation based on the similarities and/or differences discussed in the essay. For example:

- *Compare the health care systems of France and the United States. Then evaluate the more successful of the two in terms of overall public health.*

Compare and contrast essays can be organized either subject-by-subject (with particular body paragraphs discussing several points about one of the subjects, and then another body paragraph discussing the other subject) or point-by-point (with each body paragraph discussing one point about both subjects). Compare and contrast essays should discuss both subjects objectively and with equal amounts of detail for each.

Appendix B

Additional citation rules (APA style)

Below is a list of additional rules for in-text citation and References lists.

Two authors

When two authors' names are included in the sentence, use "and." When their names appear after the sentence in parentheses, use "&."

Examples:

Aisenberg and Goldade (2012) argue that simply buying fair trade goods does not solve poverty in Africa because many of the fair trade items do not even come from Africa.

Simply buying fair trade goods does not solve poverty in Africa because many of the fair trade items do not even come from Africa (Aisenberg & Goldade, 2012).

The entry on a References list for the above examples is:

Aisenberg, N., & Goldade, M. (2012). The future of fair trade: How fair can it be? *Journal of Political Geography, 29*, 139–151.

Three to five authors

When three to five authors' names are included in the sentence, use "and" before the last author. When their names appear after the sentence in parentheses, use "&" before the last author.

Examples:

Whitmore, Bay, and Henderson (2012) warn that charging the batteries to full (100%) or leaving them empty (0%) actually shortens the overall battery life of smart phones because it damages the batteries.

Charging the batteries to full (100%) or leaving them empty (0%) actually shortens the overall battery life of smart phones because it damages the batteries (Whitmore, Bay, & Henderson, 2012).

Three to five authors (subsequent citations)

When the same authors are mentioned again, write the first author's name and abbreviate the rest by using "et al."

Examples:

Accorting to Whitmore et al. (2012), using smart phones while they are charging also shortens the battery life because the heat generated while charging and using damages the batteries.

Using smart phones while they are charging also shortens the battery life because the heat generated while charging and using damages the batteries (Whitmore et al., 2012).

The entry on a References list for the preceding examples is:

Whitmore, S., Bay, F., & Henderson, J. (2012). Improving the battery life of smart phones. *Mobile Technology, 13*, 26–35.

NOTE: When there are six or more authors, do not include all the names in-text. Write only the first author's name and "et al." every time.

Acronyms

If the source is written by an organization rather than an individual author, write the full name of the organization first and include its acronym in parentheses.

Examples:

The Alliance of Concerned Parents (ACP, 2012) believes that marijuana is a gateway drug which may be less detrimental but can lead to more dangerous drugs or crimes.

Marijuana is believed to be a gateway drug which may be less detrimental but can lead to more dangerous drugs or crimes (Alliance of Concerned Parents [ACP], 2012).

Acronyms (subsequent citations)

When the same organization is mentioned again, use the acronym.

Examples:

It is reported by ACP (2012) that 50% of teenagers start smoking cigarettes for no particular reason.

Fifty percent of teenagers start smoking cigarettes for no particular reason (ACP, 2012).

The entry on a References list for the above examples is:

Alliance of Concerned Parents. (2012). Preventing drug use among high school students. Retrieved from http//www.acp.org//preventing_drug_use.html

Including a page number

When a quote is from a print source such as a book, a magazine, or a journal, indicate the page number of the source the quote came from.

Examples:

Although having had periods of great success, the fashion industry is set for more prosperous times. According to Giordano (2012), "The best days of the fashion industry may have yet to be realized with the awakening of the Asian market" (p. 29).

Although having had periods of great success, the fashion industry is set for more prosperous times. Indeed, one industry analyst claims that "the best days of the fashion industry may have yet to be realized with the awakening of the Asian market" (Giordano, 2012, p. 29).

The entry on a References list for the above examples is:

Giordano, A. (2012). *Globalizing fashion industry*. New York, NY: Vogue Publishing.

Secondhand citation

When the information used in the essay is to be found in a secondary source (a source which is written by a different author), indicate the name of the secondary source using the phrase "as cited in."

Examples:

The International Energy Agency (as cited in Nuclear Energy Institute, 2012) insists that greenhouse gas emissions over a nuclear reactor's lifecycle are actually lower than what wind or solar power would emit over a similar period at a similar wattage.

According to the International Energy Agency, greenhouse gas emissions over a nuclear reactor's lifecycle are actually lower than what wind or solar power would emit over a similar period at a similar wattage (as cited in Nuclear Energy Institute, 2012).

The entry on a References list for the above examples is:

Nuclear Energy Institute. (2012). Life-cycle emissions analysis. Retrieved from http://www.nei.org/keyissues/protectingtheenvironment/lifecycleemissionsanalysis/htm

Citing different information from the same author published in the same year

To cite information from the same author of different publications in the same year, distinguish them by adding "a, b, c ..." to the year in both the in-text citation and References list entry.

Example:

Kwon (2009a) argued for stricter environmental enforcement in the protected coastal areas. Indeed, in her keynote address at the Wetlands Conservation Plus conference, she openly criticized the local conservation authorities for their seeming unwillingness to stop illegal fishing and logging (Kwon, 2009b).

The entries on a References list for the above example are:

Kwon, J. (2009a). Dying corals: Will they be extinct in 50 years? *Journal of Marine Biology, 55*, 893–896.

Kwon, J. (2009b). Humans at the top of the food chain? Keynote presented at the Wetlands Conservation Plus Conference, Dublin, Ireland.

Source information with no dates

If the information to be cited has no date, write "n.d." in place of the year.

Examples:

California Open College (n.d.) produced an orientation pamphlet "Welcome to Academia" to further emphasize the university's zero-tolerance policy toward any academic misconduct or infraction.

The orientation pamphlet "Welcome to Academia" further emphasized the university's zero-tolerance policy toward any academic misconduct or infraction (California Open College, n.d.).

The entry on a References list for the preceding examples is:
Welcome to Academia. (n.d.). [Brochure]. San Francisco, CA: California Open College.

Synthesizing multiple sources

When two or more sources are synthesized into one paraphrase or summary, include all the sources in the in-text citation. Use a semi-colon to separate the sources in parenthesis.

Examples:
Yang (2004) and Matapang (2008) both found that students' second language acquisition was not inhibited by periodic use of their native language during class.

Two studies concluded that students' second language acquisition was not inhibited by periodic use of their native language during class (Yang, 2004; Matapang, 2008).

The entries on a References list for the above examples are:

Matapang, A. (2008). A case study of L1-use in Manila junior school English classes. *Luzon Studies in Education and Curricula*, *8*, 34–37.

Yang, T. (2004). *Additional Language Learning: The Impact of the Mother Tongue: Vol. 1*. Hong Kong: Somerset & Liu.

Unknown author

When the source is an article in a publication with no known author, use the full title of the article if it appears in the sentence. If the source is cited in parentheses, use the full title if it is short, or just the first few key words if it is long.

Examples:
According to "Solar power: A painful eclipse" (2011), the limitations of solar power prohibit it from being a viable alternative to power generated from fossil fuels.

The limitations of solar power prohibit it from being a viable alternative to power generated from fossil fuels (Solar power, 2011).

The entry on a References list for the above examples is:

Solar power: A painful eclipse. (2011, October 15). *The Economist*. Retrieved from http://www.economist.com/node/21532279

NOTE: Adding credibility and authority to the sources

Adding more information about a source to its in-text citation is not required, but doing so can increase its credibility and authority, and make the essay sound more reliable.

Examples:

According to David MacKay (2008), nuclear power produces about 760 ml of radioactive waste per person, per year, that must be securely stored for about 1,000 years.

According to Cambridge University physics professor David MacKay (2008), nuclear power produces about 760 ml of radioactive waste per person, per year, that must be securely stored for about 1,000 years.

In the above two examples, the second example indicates that the source David MacKay is a professor of physics at Cambridge University (it is underlined in this example to distinguish the information – in an essay, it would not be underlined). This additional information separates MacKay from ordinary people, and adds more credibility to the information he provides.

Appendix C

Review activity

This activity requires all aspects of a complete academic paragraph: topic sentence, waltz organization, in-text citation, reporting verbs, varied sentence types, and logical connections.

Use the information provided to write a body paragraph. The paragraph should:

- **include the paragraph theme in a topic sentence.**
- **use the paragraph ideas organized with the waltz pattern.**
- **include the source information and citation in the paragraph.**
- **include extra information from the references page entry, if desired.**
- **use effective sentences that logically connect to each other.**

Example:

Essay topic: rail travel

Paragraph theme: effects of technology on level of rail travel

Paragraph ideas:

- air travel growing popularity 1950s
- automobile – private and affordable after World War II
- travel by rail losing traditional domination
- high-speed passenger rail service spreading to many countries 1970s

Integrate the following source information as a quote:

"The development and successful application of high speed rail technologies not only revolutionized passenger train travel, but also saved it from certain extinction." Page 54

References page entry:

Porter, S. (1994). *The Last Century of Rail*. Chicago: Hope Western Publishing.

Paragraph:

Technology had a profound effect on the level of rail travel in the latter half of the twentieth century. After World War II, traveling by automobile and air became increasingly popular. This growing popularity threatened traditional rail travel, the dominant form of transport until then. However, as Porter (1994) emphasizes in *The Last Century of Rail*, "The development and successful application of high speed rail technologies not only revolutionized passenger train travel, but also saved it from certain extinction" (p. 54). Now, due to this success, high-speed passenger rail travel has been spreading worldwide since the 1970s.

1

Essay topic: the effect of Europeans on Native Americans

Paragraph theme: horses

Paragraph ideas:

- horse introduced to North America in sixteenth century
- quick impact
- Indian tribes living on plains especially influenced
- could move more easily, expand territory
- could hunt and fight more effectively

On a separate piece of paper, paraphrase the following source information and integrate it in the paragraph:

Eighteenth century French explorers recorded their great surprise that every plains Indian tribe they encountered had fully integrated horses into their way of life.

References page entry:

Morrison, H. (2009). *Post Columbus America: Western Ways and the Native Peoples*. St. Louis: Tynes and Mackie Ltd.

2

Essay topic: comparison of the ancient and modern Olympics

Paragraph theme: similarity

Paragraph ideas:

- ancient and modern Olympics not always different
- ancient games – high status for victors – very competitive
- ancient athletes look for advantages to win – used drugs
- athletics unchanged – performance enhancing drugs always present

On a separate piece of paper, integrate the following source information as a quote:

"Such is their desire for glory and riches, Olympic Games athletes eat bread containing potentially dangerous juice of the plant poppy opium, or potions made from a plant called hippouris for muscle mass and increased strength." Page 75

Quote is by the Greek philosopher Filostratos (third century BC) from his work *Gymnasticos.*

References page entry:

Stamkos, B. (2004). The game that never changes – Legal and illegal performance enhancing drugs in sport. *Journal of Recreation*, *9*(16), 74–83.

3

Essay topic: the modern wireless society

Paragraph theme: working mothers maintain careers

Paragraph ideas:

- traditionally, women sacrifice important part of life – careers – when children born – doing both not effective and very difficult
- modern wireless society – can provide women with control over lives – create better work-life balance people want

On a separate piece of paper, synthesize the following information from two different sources into one summary and integrate it into a paragraph:

In the survey, mothers who worked at home an average of 2.8 days per week using a wireless device reported they were happier working from home because they could be with their children, and felt they were more productive with their jobs.

References page entry for above information:

Jornada, E., Ng, A., & Reger, T. (2012). A study of stay at home mothers maintaining their careers. *Career and Culture*. Retrieved from http://www.carandcul.or.be/arch/23rft5/87bvt19.htm

In the study of women whose employers allowed wireless connection from home, 62% said they were significantly or somewhat more productive even with their children at home; 87% said they were much happier working from home with their children.

References page entry for above information:

Elliot, K., Marr, D., Nguyen, D., De Tina, A., Tan, V., Schopenhauer, F., & Cleary, W. (2013). The changing face of the workplace. *Studies in Social and Technological Interaction*, *34*(2), 114–120.

4

Essay topic: results of economic development on developing countries

Paragraph theme: changes in Indian social stratification

Paragraph ideas:

- young associate with people to get economic opportunities
- birth privilege less important now
- personal merit required
- economic class system replacing caste system

On a separate piece of paper, paraphrase the following source information and integrate it in the paragraph:

"A recent survey found that 84% of business owners, entrepreneurs, and managers under 40 years of age said that skill, intelligence, ambition, and proven business success, not caste, were the only factors influencing hiring people or partnering with them."

References page entry:

Chatterjee, V. (2009, October 14). The new path to losing our old path. *Asia – International Gazette*, p. C2.

5

Essay topic: threats to marine ecosystems

Paragraph theme: need to protect coral reefs

Paragraph ideas:

- important for marine life and humans
- even small changes in ecosystem – sometimes big effects huge
  diversity of marine life live in coral reefs – loss or damage of so many species could have broad-ranging impacts on the ocean
- humans need reefs – their loss would be a huge blow to a number of industries.

On a separate piece of paper, integrate the following source information as a quote:

"Coral reefs are the rainforest of the sea. Over 25% of fish in the ocean and as many as two million marine species live in or depend on coral reefs for survival." Page 93

Quote is from Pauline Santos, head biologist at the Pacific Conservation Institute.

References page entry for above information:

Foster, D. (2012). *Marine life in danger*. San Francisco: Pelican.

Paraphrase the following information and integrate it into the paragraph:

Tropical coral reefs have an estimated value of $30 to $40 billion every year. They provide food and medicine, create tourism, and prevent damage to coastlines. The local economies of many communities in developing countries in particular rely on reefs for their survival.

References page entry for above information:

Obingwe, D. (2010). Assessing the impact of human activity on reef sustainability. Retrieved from http://www.coral.research.org/obingwe.htm